Roosevelt and the New Deal

Titles in the World History Series

The Age of Augustus
The Age of Feudalism
The Age of Pericles
The Alamo
America in the 1960s
The American Frontier
The American Revolution
Ancient Greece
The Ancient Near East
Architecture
Aztec Civilization
The Battle of the
   Little Bighorn
The Black Death
The Byzantine Empire
Caesar's Conquest of Gaul
The California Gold Rush
The Chinese Cultural
   Revolution
The Civil Rights Movement
The Collapse of the
   Roman Republic
The Conquest of Mexico
The Crimean War
The Crusades
The Cuban Missile Crisis
The Cuban Revolution
The Early Middle Ages
Egypt of the Pharaohs
Elizabethan England
The End of the Cold War
The French and Indian War
The French Revolution
The Glorious Revolution
The Great Depression
Greek and Roman
   Mythology
Greek and Roman Science

Greek and Roman Theater
The History of Slavery
Hitler's Reich
The Hundred Years' War
The Industrial Revolution
The Inquisition
The Italian Renaissance
The Late Middle Ages
The Lewis and Clark
   Expedition
The Mexican Revolution
The Mexican War of
   Independence
Modern Japan
The Mongol Empire
The Persian Empire
The Punic Wars
The Reformation
The Relocation of the
   North American Indian
The Renaissance
The Roaring Twenties
The Roman Empire
The Roman Republic
Roosevelt and the New Deal
The Russian Revolution
Russia of the Tsars
The Scientific Revolution
The Spread of Islam
The Stone Age
Traditional Africa
Traditional Japan
The Travels of Marco Polo
Twentieth Century Science
The Wars of the Roses
The Watts Riot
Women's Suffrage

WORLD HISTORY SERIES ■ ■ ■

Roosevelt and the New Deal

by
Adam Woog

Lucent Books, P.O. Box 289011, San Diego, CA 92198-9011

In memory of my Grandmother

Library of Congress Cataloging-in-Publication Data

Woog, Adam, 1953–
    Roosevelt and the New Deal / by Adam Woog.
        p. cm.—(World history series)
    Includes bibliographical references and index.
    Summary: Examines the policies and programs developed
by Franklin Roosevelt to lead the country out of the Depression.
    ISBN 1-56006-324-6 (alk. paper)
    1. United States—Politics and government—1933–1945—
Juvenile literature. 2. Roosevelt, Franklin D. (Franklin Delano),
1882–1945—Juvenile literature. 3. New Deal, 1933–1939—Juvenile literature. [1. Roosevelt, Franklin D. (Franklin Delano),
1882–1945. 2. Presidents. 3. New Deal, 1933–1939. 4. United
States—Politics and government—1933–1945.]
I.Title. II. Series.
E806.W69   1998
973.917—dc21   97-27262
                                                              CIP
                                                               AC

Copyright 1998 by Lucent Books, Inc., P.O. Box 289011, San
Diego, California 92198-9011

Printed in the U.S.A.

Contents

Foreword

Each year on the first day of school, nearly every history teacher faces the task of explaining why his or her students should study history. One logical answer to this question is that exploring what happened in our past explains how the things we often take for granted—our customs, ideas, and institutions—came to be. As statesman and historian Winston Churchill put it, "Every nation or group of nations has its own tale to tell. Knowledge of the trials and struggles is necessary to all who would comprehend the problems, perils, challenges, and opportunities which confront us today." Thus, a study of history puts modern ideas and institutions in perspective. For example, though the founders of the United States were talented and creative thinkers, they clearly did not invent the concept of democracy. Instead, they adapted some democratic ideas that had originated in ancient Greece and with which the Romans, the British, and others had experimented. An exploration of these cultures, then, reveals their very real connection to us through institutions that continue to shape our daily lives.

Another reason often given for studying history is the idea that lessons exist in the past from which contemporary societies can benefit and learn. This idea, although controversial, has always been an intriguing one for historians. Those who agree that society can benefit from the past often quote philosopher George Santayana's famous statement, "Those who cannot remember the past are condemned to repeat it." Historians who ascribe to Santayana's philosophy believe that, for

example, studying the events that led up to the major world wars or other significant historical events would allow society to chart a different and more favorable course in the future.

Just as difficult as convincing students to realize the importance of studying history is the search for useful and interesting supplementary materials that present historical events in a context that can be easily understood. The volumes in Lucent Books' World History Series attempt to present a broad, balanced, and penetrating view of the march of history. Ancient Egypt's important wars and rulers, for example, are presented against the rich and colorful backdrop of Egyptian religious, social, and cultural developments. The series engages the reader by enhancing historical events with these cultural contexts. For example, in *Ancient Greece*, the text covers the role of women in that society. Slavery is discussed in *The Roman Empire*, as well as how slaves earned their freedom. The numerous and varied aspects of everyday life in these and other societies are explored in each volume of the series. Additionally, the series covers the major political, cultural, and philosophical ideas as the torch of civilization is passed from ancient Mesopotamia and Egypt, through Greece, Rome, Medieval Europe, and other world cultures, to the modern day.

The material in the series is formatted in a thorough, precise, and organized manner. Each volume offers the reader a comprehensive and clearly written overview of an important historical event or period. The topic under discussion is placed in a broad historical context. For example, *The Italian Renaissance* begins with a discussion of the High Middle Ages and the loss of central control that allowed certain Italian cities to develop artistically. The book ends by looking forward to the Reformation and interpreting the societal changes that grew out of the Renaissance. Thus, students are not only involved in an historical era, but also enveloped by the events leading up to that era and the events following it.

One important and unique feature in the World History Series is the primary and secondary source quotations that richly supplement each volume. These quotes are useful in a number of ways. First, they allow students access to sources they would not normally be exposed to because of the difficulty and obscurity of the original source. The quotations range from interesting anecdotes to farsighted cultural perspectives and are drawn from historical witnesses both past and present. Second, the quotes demonstrate how and where historians themselves derive their information on the past as they strive to reach a consensus on historical events. Lastly, all of the

quotes are footnoted, familiarizing students with the citation process and allowing them to verify quotes and/or look up the original source if the quote piques their interest.

Finally, the books in the World History Series provide a detailed launching point for further research. Each book contains a bibliography specifically geared toward student research. A second, annotated bibliography introduces students to all the sources the author consulted when compiling the book. A chronology of important dates gives students an overview, at a glance, of the topic covered. Where applicable, a glossary of terms is included.

In short, the series is designed not only to acquaint readers with the basics of history, but also to make them aware that their lives are a part of an ongoing human saga. Perhaps they will then come to the same realization as famed historian Arnold Toynbee. In his monumental work, *A Study of History,* he wrote about becoming aware of history flowing through him in a mighty current, and of his own life "welling like a wave in the flow of this vast tide."

Important Dates in the History of the New Deal

1882   1910   1913   1921   1929   1931   1935   1937   1938   1940   1941   1944   1945

1882
Franklin Delano Roosevelt is born on January 30 in Hyde Park, New York.

1910
FDR wins first election, to the New York State Senate.

1913
FDR is appointed assistant secretary of the navy.

1921
FDR is stricken with polio.

1929
FDR is inaugurated as governor of New York; the U.S. stock market crashes on October 29, marking the beginning of the Great Depression.

1932
The expulsion by government troops of the Bonus Army in Washington becomes a rallying point against President Herbert Hoover's inability to fix the problems of the depression; FDR wins the presidential election over Hoover.

1933
Roosevelt is inaugurated on March 4 as the thirty-second president of the United States.

March–June
The Hundred Days of legislative action in Congress creates many new bills and agencies to combat the depression, including the Emergency Banking Relief Act, the Civilian Conservation Corps, the Federal Emergency Relief Act, the Agricultural Adjustment Act, the Federal Deposit Insurance Corporation, the Tennessee Valley Authority, the Home Owners Refinancing Act, and the National Industrial Recovery Act.

1934
Securities Exchange Act passed; Securities and Exchange Commission created.

1935
Works Progress Administration is created; the U.S. Supreme Court declares the National Industrial Recovery Act unconstitutional; National Labor Relations Act and Social Security Act are passed.

1936
Roosevelt wins a second term of office.

1937
FDR introduces his disastrous "court-packing" scheme.

1938
Congress passes the last major reform law of the New Deal, the Fair Labor Standards Act.

1940
Roosevelt wins a third term of office.

1941
Attack on Pearl Harbor by Japanese forces marks the U.S. entrance into World War II and the effective end of the New Deal.

1944
FDR wins a fourth term of office.

1945
FDR dies on April 12 at Warm Springs, Georgia.

A New Deal for America

Roosevelt, optimistic by nature, never doubted the mission of the American people and their great destiny.

historian Frank Freidel

The Roaring Twenties was an era of good times for most Americans. There were plenty of jobs, the economy was strong, entertainments such as public dancing were more popular than ever, and new technology like the radio, the refrigerator, and the movies helped make life easier and more enjoyable. This period of easy living was a

During the height of the Great Depression, a farmworker and his family live in desperate poverty at a migrant camp.

welcome relief after the hard years of 1914–1918, when America had helped its allies fight World War I in Europe.

Late in 1929, however, the country's booming economy suddenly collapsed. The period that followed, the Great Depression, was the worst economic disaster in American history. For nearly a decade afterward, millions of people suffered from scarcity—scarcity of adequate jobs, homes, medical care, and even food.

At the depression's lowest point, one-fourth of the nation's workforce—about thirteen million people—had no jobs. When they could find work, it was not always enough. Meanwhile, housewives went to work outside the home in large numbers for the first time, and children quit school early to find jobs. Households doubled up to save on rent, families took in lodgers, and homeless people wandered the roads. "There were many beggars, who would come to your front door," one housewife recalls, "and they would say they were hungry. I wouldn't give them money because I didn't have it. But I did take them in and put them in my kitchen and give them something to eat."[1]

In the early years of the crisis, the nation's president, Herbert Hoover, failed to pull America out of this misery. The small steps he took were not effective, and be-

"Like the Drounding Man"

The starvation conditions during the worst of the depression were unlike any others in American history, as this excerpt from Franklin D. Roosevelt and the New Deal *illustrates.*

"'We are like the drounding man, grabbing at every thing that flotes by, trying to save what little we have,' reported a North Carolinian. In Chicago, a crowd of some fifty hungry men fought over a barrel of garbage set outside the back door of a restaurant; in Stockton, California, men scoured the city dump near the San Joaquin River to retrieve half-rotted vegetables. . . . 'We have been eating wild greens,' wrote a coal miner from Kentucky's Harlan County. 'Such as Polk salad, Violet tops, wild onions, forget me not wild lettuce and such weeds as cows eat as a cow wont eat a poison weeds.'"

cause he feared that major programs of government assistance would make citizens lazy, he ruled out broader relief measures. Thus, the country sank further into poverty, and many people doubted that the prosperous times would ever return.

The tide turned when a dynamic new leader emerged on the scene. Franklin Delano Roosevelt, the governor of New York State, had unstoppable faith in Americans' ability to recover their standard of living if the government took quick and vigorous action. This reassuring confidence struck a chord in voters, and when Roosevelt ran for president in 1932 on the Democratic ticket, he won by a landslide.

A New Deal

Roosevelt was elected on the strength of his promise to enact a sweeping set of programs and policies designed to strength-

en the economy and relieve widespread poverty. In his inaugural speech in 1933, he spoke of these plans as "a new deal." This phrase immediately became a source of both inspiration and controversy.

Roosevelt's New Deal did not completely eliminate the depression. It did, however, provide much immediate good. It put millions of people to work, provided greatly needed assistance for millions more, and created programs that strengthened the economy. In addition, financial rules and regulations were established to prevent another devastating economic collapse.

There were other effects of the New Deal as well. Before Roosevelt, the federal government provided no social security or unemployment insurance to Americans who were elderly, sick, or out of a job. It did not lend a hand to low-income families or first-time home owners. Nor did it provide protection from unscrupulous business practices: before Roosevelt, there

Untraditional Hoboes

Nearly two million men wandered the country during the depression in search of the paradise that a popular song called "the Big Rock Candy Mountain." An excerpt from Franklin D. Roosevelt and the New Deal *describes the scene.*

"They roved the waterfronts of both oceans, rode in cattle cars and gondolas of the Rock Island and the Southern Pacific, slept on benches in Boston Common and Lafayette Square, in Chicago's Grant Park and El Paso's Plaza. From Klamath Falls to Sparks to Yuma, they shared the hobo's quarters in oak thickets strewn with blackened cans along the railroad tracks. . . . Unlike the traditional hobo, they sought not to evade work but to find it. But it was a dispirited search. They knew they were not headed toward the Big Rock Candy Mountain; they were not, in fact, headed anywhere, only fleeing from where they had been."

were no regulations of the stock market, no bank insurance, no laws establishing minimum wages or forbidding child labor, no rules about fair advertising, and no building safety codes.

The New Deal changed all that, and so permanently changed the relationship between Americans and their government. Roosevelt's belief—and the basis of the New Deal—was that all citizens had a right to a minimum standard of living. His administration firmly established, for the first time in America, the principle that the federal government has certain basic duties to these citizens.

Roosevelt's beliefs and the policies he set are controversial even today. Ideas about welfare and the proper amount of government control over business and private lives are still topics of debate. Many current agencies that deal with these issues are direct descendants of New Deal agencies. From the Department of Health and Human Services to the Environmental Protection Agency and the National Endowment for the Arts, these organizations and their policies still arouse passionate defense as well as severe criticism.

Leading the Country

The New Deal was created by many individuals and groups. Presidential advisers, various politicians, and others influenced the decisions of the man who would become known the world over as FDR. Still, to many people, Roosevelt and the New Deal were one and the same. People who disliked the New Deal generally hated the man; those who thought the man was a savior generally loved the New Deal. In many ways, the story of the New Deal is also FDR's story.

In the years following his presidential victory in 1932, FDR became one of the most popular and even beloved leaders in American history. One measure of this popularity is that he was the first—and only—president to be elected to a third and fourth term in office. In part this popularity was due to the changes he brought to ease the miseries of the Great Depression and in part by his leadership during a later crisis, World War II.

To a great degree, however, Roosevelt's appeal lay in his personality, in his ability to soothe anxious nerves while taking decisive action. He developed an easy and trusting relationship with ordinary people during his many travels and frequent radio talks. One insurance salesman, when asked by an interviewer about Roosevelt's appeal, replied, "My mother looks upon the President as someone so immediately concerned with her problems and difficulties that she would not be greatly surprised were he to come to her house some evening and stay to dinner."[2]

At the same time, many voters and politicians disliked and distrusted FDR.

Franklin D. Roosevelt (above and below) was such a popular president that he was elected to an unprecedented fourth term. Much of his popularity was due to his commitment to helping those in need.

Someone Who Understood

This excerpt from Robert McElvaine's The Great Depression *suggests that Roosevelt's struggle with polio had a dramatic effect on his character and on his immense popularity.*

"Determined always to succeed in politics, FDR had nonetheless been something of a carefree playboy before his paralysis. He seems to have become inwardly more serious afterward. Most of all, Roosevelt's suffering helped to broaden his patrician sense of stewardship [aristocratic attitude toward helping the poor] into a more genuine sense of compassion. . . .

This was absolutely critical to Roosevelt's later relationship with victims of the Great Depression. . . . He was able to understand suffering in a way a [rich landowner] would not have otherwise been likely to. And, to the deprived, the smiling . . . attitude Roosevelt took in the face of the Depression was acceptable and uplifting only because he had overcome a terrible affliction himself. Without this 'blessing in disguise,' Roosevelt's jauntiness in the thirties would likely have turned people against him as an overprivileged man who did not understand life's hardships."

He was a smooth politician with a gift for being maddeningly vague about specifics, and he was a tough negotiator who worked tirelessly with differing groups to find compromise solutions. The laws that came out of these battles often angered as many people as they pleased. Where some saw an inspiring leader whose policies represented enlightened democracy at its best, others saw an arrogant authoritarian who abused the powers of his office and embraced dangerously radical ideas.

The truth, perhaps, lies somewhere in between. Roosevelt the man had his faults, and the New Deal fell short of expectations. Nonetheless, FDR and his programs had an enormous impact on American history and politics. His jaunty confidence in himself, and in America, helped lift the spirits of a disheartened nation. His policies, meanwhile, provided bold experiments that did much to bring the country back to prosperity and set the course of future policy.

An editorial in the British newspaper *The Economist*—published in 1940, midway through Roosevelt's terms of office—emphasizes the confident vigor that characterized the New Deal and its creator. "Mr. Roosevelt may have given the wrong answers" to many of the depression's problems, the editorial asserts. "But he is at least the first President of modern America who has asked the right questions."[3]

Chapter

1 Before the New Deal: The Great Depression

Yes, it was called the Dark Ages, and it lasted four hundred years.

> economist John Maynard Keynes, when asked if the world had ever seen anything like the Great Depression

Before the Great Depression, America had enjoyed one of the longest and largest economic booms in the country's history. Early in 1929, when Franklin D. Roosevelt became governor of New York and Herbert Hoover became America's thirty-first president, factories were running at full capacity and farms were abundantly productive. Unemployment was at an all-time low. Prices on the stock market had risen to unprecedented heights.

Millions of people were still at the poverty level, but, on the whole, the economy seemed secure and prosperous. Credit made it easy to buy new things, and Americans everywhere were snapping up millions of big-ticket items like cars as well as smaller luxuries, such as radios and refrigerators. Herbert Hoover, in accepting the Republican presidential nomination in 1928, had summed up the national mood when he proclaimed, "We in America today are nearer to the final triumph over poverty than ever before in the history of any land."[4]

Late in 1929, the bubble burst.

There had been hints for some time that the economy was in trouble. One worrisome statistic was the drop in construction starts—that is, the building of new houses. This common measure of economic stability had been declining sharply for the three years prior to 1929. Other factors contributing to the overall down-

This photograph epitomizes the glamour and prosperity of the 1920s. The woman's fashionable clothes and sporty roadster are emblematic of the decade's economic optimism.

Hundreds gather at the New York Stock Exchange after news of the 1929 crash.

invested heavily in the market saw their savings wiped out.

The exact causes of the stock market crash of 1929 are still being debated. Most experts agree, however, that a major factor was the misuse of credit: brokers had charged billions of dollars' worth of stock to so-called margin accounts. There were no safeguards to prevent this practice, which worked smoothly only when prices were rising or relatively stable. If prices fell sharply, brokers who could not raise large sums of money to "meet margin calls"— that is, cover or pay their debts—lost their entire investment.

The Great Depression

The stock market crash was the most serious sign yet of a major economic downturn. Periods of downward financial trends are called recessions. Severe and long-lasting recessions are called depressions. Both recessions and depressions occur periodically and are considered fairly normal events in economics.

In many cases, the economy stabilizes quickly after a downturn and rises again rapidly. President Hoover predicted that this would happen after Black Thursday; he was confident that the crisis was temporary. He and his advisers felt that the downturn needed to "run its natural course" and correct itself.

The economy did not spring back, however, and within a few months panic had spread from Wall Street across the country. Increasing numbers of nervous consumers, businessmen, and investors were unwilling or unable to buy appliances, materials for manufacturing, or any-

turn, such as lower profits in key industries such as coal, textiles, and railroads, were largely overlooked by those who were enjoying the boom.

Although some economists had pointed to such signs as heralding an economic crisis, many people, from influential politicians and bankers to ordinary consumers, ignored them. Then came October 24, 1929, a date now known as Black Thursday. On that day, prices on the New York Stock Exchange suddenly plummeted. Brokers on Wall Street panicked, frantically selling off their most valuable assets at fractions of the original prices. Within five days, trading in stocks and bonds collapsed entirely. People who had thing else. Less spending meant less production and, as production slowed, people lost their jobs.

In cities, factory production fell to half its former level. In rural areas, farming families were faced with the loss of land that had been theirs for generations. By mid-1930, four million out of about fifty million eligible Americans were unemployed. This figure, slightly less than 10 percent, was shocking to a nation accustomed to a much lower jobless rate. (Official statistics on unemployment were not kept in the United States until later years, but the pre-Crash unemployment figure was probably at most only a few percentage points.)

Some people responded to the hard times with complete despair, and the national suicide rate began rising. Others were attracted to political philosophies that advocated sweeping change, such as anarchy, communism, and socialism. The majority of Americans, however, simply

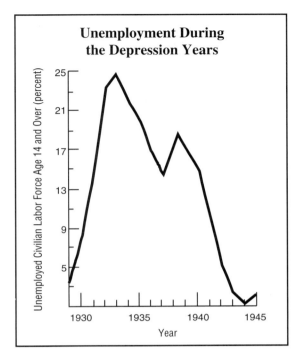

Unemployment During the Depression Years

seemed resigned to a sad fate, or as historian William E. Leuchtenberg writes, "The country was less rebellious than drifting."[5]

Sad but Not Rebellious

In The Great Depression, *Robert McElvaine quotes three comments that illustrate the quiet resignation many Americans felt during the hard times.*

"Marquis Childs [a respected journalist] wrote in January 1933: 'What is surprising is the passive resignation with which the blow has been accepted. . . .'

[Writer and historian] Louis Adamic, speaking of American workers, wrote in 1931: 'I have a definite feeling that millions of them, now that they are unemployed, are licked.' The *New Yorker* [then as now a source of thoughtful commentary on the national scene] summed up the contemporary view in mid-1931: 'People are in a sad, but not a rebellious mood.'"

Unemployed men sit on a park bench in attitudes of hopelessness and exhaustion in this 1934 photograph.

Brother, Can You Spare a Dime?

The situation continued to worsen throughout the early 1930s, and signs of desperation were everywhere.

Crowds fought over barrels of garbage set out behind restaurants. Children were kept from school because their families were ashamed to send them out in public without decent clothes. Bread lines for the needy stretched for blocks, and soup kitchens set up by local agencies or religious charities handed out what they could: weak coffee and skimpy, not very nourishing meals.

One Philadelphia storekeeper told a reporter about a family he was supporting by extending them credit: "Eleven children in that house. They've got no shoes, no pants. In the house, no chairs. My God, you go in there, you cry, that's all."[6]

American women had rarely worked outside the home, but now they took in laundry or did anything else they could to supplement household incomes. Millions of men left their homes and wandered the country searching for work. They hitchhiked, rode in boxcars, slept on park benches, shared makeshift hobo jungles along railroad tracks.

In big cities and small towns, homeless families lived in thrown-together shacks made of boxes and scrap metal. Vacant lots began to fill with these makeshift shelters. With a bitter wit directed at the man they blamed for it all, the residents of the shantytowns called them "Hoovervilles."

One of the most dramatic symbols of the nation's despair was the street-side apple seller. Early in the Great Depression, the

International Apple Shippers Association came up with a way to dispose of its surplus fruit. The organization sold the apples to jobless people, who sold them on the street for five cents each. Soon, apple sellers could be seen on street corners everywhere.

The era's popular songs reflected these hard times. While some tunes like "We're in the Money" tried to overcome gloom with bright optimism, others were darker and sadder, like this 1932 hit:

> They used to tell me I was building a
>   dream
> With peace and glory ahead
> Why should I be standing in line
> Just waiting for bread?

Once I built a railroad, made it run
Made it race against time
Once I built a railroad, now it's done
Brother, can you spare a dime? [7]

Vibrations but Not Tone

For the most part, Americans were on their own when it came to finding relief. A few European countries had long-established programs for the needy and unemployed, such as Germany, Sweden, and Great Britain, which in 1911 became the first country to adopt national unemployment

Americans responded to the Great Depression by becoming ingenious at finding ways to make money. At left, a sign proclaims that this woman will take in laundry. At right, a man sells apples on the street.

"A Bit Outraged, Too"

E. Y. (Yip) Harburg wrote the lyrics to a song that summed up the anger, sadness, and frustration many people felt during the depression years: "Brother, Can You Spare a Dime?" In this passage from Studs Terkel's Hard Times, *Harburg recalls the emotions that led to his composition, which was a powerful anthem of the era.*

"We thought American business was the Rock of Gibraltar. We were a prosperous nation, and nothing could stop us now. . . . Suddenly the big dream exploded. The impact was unbelievable.

I was walking along the street at that time, and you'd see the bread lines. . . . Fellows with burlap on their shoes were lined up all around Columbus Circle [in New York], and went on for blocks and blocks around the park, waiting. . . .

[H]ow do you do a song so it isn't maudlin [overly sentimental]? Not to say: my wife is sick, I've got six children, the Crash put me out of business, hand me a dime. I hate songs of that kind. . . .

In the song the man is really saying: I made an investment in this country. Where the hell are my dividends? . . . It doesn't reduce him to a beggar. It makes him a dignified human, asking questions—and a bit outraged, too, as he should be."

insurance and, in the following year, also made health insurance compulsory. The American tradition, however, had always been one of self-help.

Hoover was reluctant to underwrite federal programs to dispense money to individuals and families in the form of transfer payments—that is, welfare, jobless benefits, medical aid, subsidized housing, and other forms of assistance. During and after World War I, Hoover had earned a reputation as an able, compassionate administrator of European relief efforts. In general, however, he believed that individuals, local governments, and private charitable organizations should bear the responsibility of assisting the unfortunate.

A self-made millionaire, Hoover believed in the virtues of hard work and self-reliance. He feared that government handouts would destroy these characteristics in the American people. Anyone, he felt, could pull him- or herself up by the bootstraps. "If a man has not made a million dollars by the time he is forty," Hoover once remarked, "he is not worth much."[8] Such exaggerated statements by public figures were taken with a grain of salt, but they did indicate the speakers' basic attitudes.

In the past, local agencies and private charities had been able to care for the needy in their communities. As the depression deepened, however, the situation was far too drastic for established organizations. They simply had too little in the way of money, manpower, and resources to handle the number of families who needed help. Frank Murphy, the mayor of Detroit, remarked that the dilemma he faced was to "feed half the people or half-feed the people."[9]

Hoover and his advisers were more inclined to give help to business than to individuals, on the theory that a strong business scene helped everyone. This theory, known as trickle-down economics, called for the government to lend money to banks. The banks would then lend money to business and industry, which would put laid-off employees back to work. Money would thus trickle down to the majority of people.

To put this theory into effect, Hoover did several things. He formed the Recon-

A cartoon pokes fun at Hoover's farm relief plan, decrying it as nothing more than a scarecrow—easy prey for the birds labeled hard times.

Herbert Hoover tried a traditionally conservative but slow method of alleviating the depression when his administration lent money to businesses in the hopes that they would use it to employ workers.

struction Finance Corporation, which made loans to financial institutions, local governments, and certain businesses, such as railroads, which had been in trouble for some time. He also encouraged businessmen to keep wages high and began a limited program to create federally funded jobs.

In the opinion of many, however, these measures were too little and too late. Furthermore, they angered average Americans, who could not understand how the government justified giving millions to railroads while refusing to provide food for starving families. Critics accused Hoover of doing nothing to help the average person.

Hoover was hindered by his personal manner, which was not one of warmth or humor. Voters increasingly saw him as an uncaring bureaucrat with an engineer's tendency to consider people as statistics. Since Hoover mistrusted reporters and had little to say to them, newspapers also grew steadily more hostile. The Washington correspondent of the London *Times* wrote that the president "can calculate wavelengths, but cannot see color. . . . He can understand vibrations but cannot hear tone." Gutzon Borglum, a distinguished sculptor, added this bitter assessment: "If you put a rose in Hoover's hand, it would wilt."[10]

The Bonus Army

One controversy in particular dramatically highlighted the public's view of a cold and distant president. In 1924, several years after the end of World War I, veterans of that war had been promised bonuses for their service. These bonuses were due to be paid in 1945. As the depression deepened in the 1930s, however, many veterans began agitating for immediate payment of these funds.

In 1932 about twenty-five thousand veterans, the so-called Bonus Army, marched to Washington, D.C., to voice their demands. The city's police department allowed about eleven thousand of the soldiers to stay, and they set up a camp with their families on the Anacostia Flats across from the congressional buildings. Apart

Veterans of the Bonus Army camp outside Congress in Washington, D.C., to demand bonuses promised them during World War I.

from one incident of violence, it was a peaceful and well-maintained enclave.

The veterans denied rumors that they were inspired by communism or wanted to overthrow the government. Nonetheless, many politicians and military leaders were convinced that the Bonus Army was a serious threat to national security. Hoover eventually instructed General Douglas MacArthur to dismantle the camp. MacArthur went further, ordering an attack on the veterans and their families, which Hoover did nothing to stop.

Men, women, and children were chased from their burning shanties on the Anacostia Flats by tanks and tear gas. Newsreels shown before feature films were the most common news medium besides papers in 1932, and theater audiences across the country were shocked to see newsreel footage of soldiers attacking their former comrades. It was the final straw for many voters; historian Anthony Badger explains, "The sight of troops so thoroughly routing [dispersing] helpless, unemployed veterans, women, and children froze Hoover's uncaring image in ice."[11]

The Bonus Army would meet with a very different reception when they returned to Washington in the spring of 1934, after FDR had taken office. Then, they were greeted cordially, issued blankets and food, housed in a tent city with showers and electricity, and treated to a band concert. They were even visited by Eleanor Roosevelt, the president's wife. Roosevelt angered many veterans by still deferring their payments, but as a public relations move his treatment of the Bonus Army was the complete opposite of Hoover's. "The treatment given the two contingents was an instructive measure of the two presidents," writes historian Page

Smith. "[Roosevelt's] handling of the problem they presented was both humane and politically astute."[12]

Roosevelt Changes His Views

In the early days of the depression, when he was governor of New York, Roosevelt agreed with Hoover that the economy would correct itself quickly. In many ways, Roosevelt was an economic conservative, and, like Hoover, he was reluctant to spend large amounts of public money for relief.

The morning after Black Thursday, Governor Roosevelt sent a telegram to a New York newspaper from his second home in Warm Springs, Georgia, expressing his belief "that industrial and trade conditions are sound." Historian Frank Freidel notes:

> Through the first stages of the economic decline when conditions were not too bad, Roosevelt continued to be slow in sensing its implications or proposing means to combat it. For a year [he] favored only limited assistance to the unemployed through some expansion of public works.[13]

As things grew worse, however, Roosevelt became more aware of the need for action. He developed a plan for his state that involved vigorous government action to stimulate the economy and provide relief. Chief among these were works projects, large-scale programs that would create government-sponsored jobs, and a form of unemployment insurance that would provide an income for people during periods of joblessness.

As governor of New York during the Great Depression, Roosevelt organized a massive relief effort to put people back to work.

New York's TERA

Roosevelt's Temporary Emergency Relief Administration (TERA) made New York the first state in the nation to battle unemployment through direct government action. TERA provided jobs for the unemployed through a variety of public works and reforestation projects. The agency also directly provided food, clothing, and shelter to some needy families. By 1932 nearly one family out of ten in New York State received some form of relief from TERA.

FDR saw such measures primarily as a means to economic prosperity, but he also saw them as simple humanitarian gestures. They appealed to his sense of social justice. Although he had grown up as the only son in a wealthy and aristocratic family, he had deep empathy for ordinary people and their problems. At a conference of governors in 1931, Roosevelt declared, "More and more, those who are victims of dislocations and defects of our social and economic life are beginning to ask . . . why government can not and should not act to protect its citizens from disaster."[14]

Funding TERA had required doubling the New York State income tax, and Roosevelt's critics warned that he was bankrupting the state. Elsewhere, however, the governor was widely praised. His advocates felt he was doing more than any other politician to relieve the misery of "the forgotten man" (as FDR himself put it in numerous speeches). He became an increasingly vocal critic of Hoover's do-nothing policies; and voters and politicians across the country began to notice the charismatic governor. As Hoover faced a run for a second term in 1932, Roosevelt emerged as a major contender for the Democratic nomination.

Birth of a Phrase

Not everyone was impressed. Roosevelt's gift for rallying supporters while remaining vague about specific plans infuriated many. FDR promised to increase aid to the unemployed, for instance, while slashing the federal budget. He never explained, however, exactly how these seemingly contradictory actions could both occur.

Walter Lippmann, the most influential political columnist in America, called Roosevelt "an amiable Boy Scout" and declared that Roosevelt was

> a highly impressionable person, without a firm grasp of public affairs, and without very strong convictions. . . . He is too eager to please. . . . He is . . . a pleasant man who, without any important qualifications for the office, would very much like to be President.[15]

Nonetheless, Roosevelt was chosen as the Democratic candidate at the party's convention in Chicago that summer.

By tradition, nominees did not attend the conventions. Instead, they waited in their hometowns until they were informed by a formal delegation. Roosevelt decided to break tradition, and the results were dramatic. At a time when commercial air travel was still a dangerous adventure, he flew to Chicago and accepted in person— a move that suited his bold style. In 1910 Roosevelt had been the first politician to campaign by automobile while running for the state legislature in New York. Now he became the first presidential candidate to make a campaign trip by airplane.

During his acceptance speech, Roosevelt uttered these words:

> I pledge you, I pledge myself, to a new deal for the American people. . . . Give me your help, not to win votes alone, but to win in this crusade to restore America to its own people.[16]

The phrase "new deal" itself is generally attributed to Roosevelt's chief speechwriter, Samuel Rosenman. Some historians, however, believe that the phrase was coined by Raymond Moley, another close Roosevelt adviser. In either case, it appears that no one thought much about the phrase before the speech was delivered. It caught the imagination of reporters, however, and by the next day newspapers across the country were talking excitedly about "Roosevelt's New Deal."

Roosevelt Sweeps the Nation

The Republican Party loyally stood by its incumbent president, Herbert Hoover, and nominated him for a second term. However, even Hoover himself admitted to reporters that his chances looked slim.

In the minds of millions of Americans, Hoover had become the symbol of their hardships. His campaign was lackluster, and the candidate remained pessimistic, unfriendly, and remote. In Detroit, where unemployment was creeping toward the 50-percent mark and conditions were especially harsh, Hoover's campaign train was met by an angry mob shouting, "Hang him! Hang him!"

By comparison, Roosevelt radiated good cheer and optimism. He conducted a well-organized, physically demanding campaign, traveling constantly and delivering his positive message from the rear platform of a campaign train. One reason Roosevelt traveled so extensively was that he loved talking to crowds and gaining their confidence. He also knew the value to a politician of talking to ordinary citizens, and he genuinely enjoyed hearing their opinions on conditions and issues.

Moreover, an important part of Roosevelt's appeal was his energy, and the candidate wanted to demonstrate that he was physically able to withstand the rigors of the presidency.

As a young man, Roosevelt had been stricken with polio. It left him unable to walk without the aid of heavy iron braces and a strong arm to lean on, and he spent nearly every waking hour in a wheelchair. In those days, misunderstanding and prejudice against the disabled would have kept many citizens from voting for Roosevelt. Few people would have believed that a wheelchair-bound man possessed the stamina to lead the country.

FDR was so determined to downplay his disability that it virtually remained a secret from the public. During the campaign and all through his presidency, Roosevelt asked newspaper photographers and newsreel cameramen not to show him in his wheelchair or locking his braces prior to getting out of a car. "No movies of me getting out of the machine, boys,"[17] he would tell them. Reporters respected this request, and only a handful of photographs survive showing Roosevelt in "the machine." The stratagem was so successful that most Americans of the day were not aware of the extent of his disability.

On election day 1932, Roosevelt fulfilled his early promise as a strong campaigner. He swept the country by an enormous margin, receiving 22,800,000 votes to Hoover's 15,750,000. In the electoral college, the difference was even more striking; Roosevelt received 472 votes to Hoover's paltry 59. Roosevelt captured 42 out of the nation's 48 states and carried more counties than any previous candidate in history.

Democrats also won significant gains in the congressional elections held that year. Overall, it was an unbelievable land-

Speaking from his campaign train in 1932, FDR communicates his message of optimism to a nation weary of Hoover's policies.

The Need for Action

Historian Arthur M. Schlesinger Jr., in this excerpt from The Politics of Upheaval, *emphasizes how important and necessary decisive measures were to lift the country from its doldrums on the eve of FDR's inauguration.*

"It was hard to understate the need for action. The national income was less than half of what it had been four short years before. Nearly thirteen million Americans—about one quarter of the labor force—were desperately seeking jobs. The machinery for sheltering and feeding the unemployed was breaking down everywhere under the growing burden. And a few hours before, in the early morning before the inauguration, every bank in America had locked its doors. It was now not just a matter of staving off hunger. It was a matter of seeing whether a representative democracy could conquer economic collapse. It was a matter of staving off violence, even (at least some so thought) revolution."

slide for the Democrats and one of the worst defeats in Republican history.

Waiting

Once the euphoria of the victory died, however, the president-elect faced the grim reality of preparing to lead a country where one-fourth of the workforce had no jobs. The months between Roosevelt's election in November and his inauguration in March were long and painful, as the nation waited restlessly before its new leader could take action.

This period was so difficult that the inaugural date was later changed from March to January, shortening the period between the November election and the start of a new administration. The days before Roosevelt took power, according to historian Shelley Bookspan, were "among the bleakest of the depression":

> As food prices fell dramatically, armed and angry farmers defended their property from repossessors. Beggars in record numbers took to the city streets; vagabonds took to the highways; families were separated. . . . Spending sagged. Banks failed. Congress stuttered. Americans trembled from cold, hunger, and fear.[18]

The interregnum, as this period was known, was mercifully only a few months in duration. Soon, Roosevelt's New Deal policies would be sweeping America.

2 "The Only Thing We Have to Fear Is Fear Itself": The New Deal Is Born

This nation is asking for action, and action now.

Franklin D. Roosevelt

Franklin Delano Roosevelt was sworn in as the thirty-second president of the United States on March 4, 1933. The crowd that gathered to witness the event covered forty acres around the Capitol building, eager to see the new leader who was promising so much. Referring to FDR's distant relative, war hero and president Theodore Roosevelt, historian Robert McElvaine writes, "Many were looking for a hero to save the nation. Teddy had been a hero; why not another Roosevelt?"[19]

After reciting the oath of office with Supreme Court chief justice Charles Evans Hughes, FDR wasted no time in delivering his message, an eloquent speech that did much to begin moving the national spirit from gloom to hope. Perhaps more than any of Roosevelt's many addresses to the nation, it symbolized his unshakable confidence that a new era was about to begin. In this speech, Roosevelt voiced words that are among his most famous: "The only thing we have to fear is fear itself—

FDR is sworn in as president on March 4, 1933. His inaugural speech is still remembered today for its stirring message.

"My Friends!"

An unnamed reporter for Time *sketched the scene of Roosevelt's 1933 inauguration on the steps of the Capitol building. The piece is reprinted in an anniversary issue of* Time, *October 5, 1983.*

"Ta-ta-Ta-ta-aa sounded a bugle. Through the great bronze doors that tell the story of Columbus, appeared the President-elect leaning on the arm of his son James. From the door to the platform had been built a special ramp, carpeted in maroon. Down this he shuffled slowly while the crowd cheered and the Marine Band played 'Hail to the Chief.'

President Roosevelt, without hat or overcoat in the chill wind, swung around to the crowd before him, launched vigorously into his inaugural address. His easy smile was gone. His large chin was thrust out defiantly as if at some invisible, insidious foe. A challenge rang in his clear strong voice. For 20 vibrant minutes he held his audience, seen and unseen, under a strong spell.

'My friends!' he began. 'This is a day of national consecration. . . . The only thing we have to fear is fear itself—nameless, unreasoning, unjustified terror which paralyzes needed efforts to convert retreat into advance.

'This nation asks for action, and action now. Our greatest primary task is to put people to work. It can be accomplished in part by direct recruiting by the Government itself, treating the task as we would treat the emergency of a war.'"

nameless, unreasoning, unjustified terror which paralyzes needed efforts to convert retreat into advance."[20]

The Banking Crisis

Roosevelt's most immediate task was to stop the panic in America's banking system, which was causing thousands of banks to close. Although the situation had been brewing for some time, it did not reach a crisis point until the last days of Hoover's administration. First a few small banks in severely depressed rural areas were forced to close. Then panicky citizens elsewhere began withdrawing their savings in fear that otherwise the money would be lost. These so-called runs on banks were symbolized by long lines outside banks, as depositors waited and hoped that there would still be money on hand when it was their turn to demand immediate payment.

A local bank is closed during the depression. One of FDR's first moves as president was to close all of the banks, allowing only those that were solvent to reopen.

Most of the banks' assets, however, were frozen in loans that would never be repaid. Since borrowers had lost all their money, their property, and valuables, there was nothing left for the banks to seize in repayment. Thus, most financial institutions had very little cash on hand. Unable to give depositors their money, more and more banks were forced to close.

As Roosevelt took office, over five thousand banks, nearly a quarter of all the banks in America, had shut down. Thousands more were on the brink of collapse, and tens of thousands of individuals had already lost their savings.

The banking crisis affected a wide range of other businesses, including the stock market and mortgage companies. The U.S. Treasury did not even have enough money to meet the government payroll. The country was not yet in danger of complete economic collapse, but, as Anthony Badger notes, "the financial and credit system of the United States had come to a halt."[21]

The Bank Holiday

In his approach to the bank crisis, Roosevelt acted conservatively. Within days of his inauguration, he put into action a temporary plan that Hoover's administration had developed: a national banking holiday that closed the banks for four days.

Roosevelt hoped this would prevent further runs on banks, giving the government time to release federal money to help banks meet future runs. It would also give him time to rally the nervous public and calm their panic-driven desire to withdraw their savings.

FDR summoned the House and Senate into a special session, and Congress took remarkably swift action. The bill Roosevelt was proposing to make into law, the Emergency Banking Relief Act, had been drafted so hastily that no copies were available for members of Congress to study. Instead, one clerk read aloud from the only copy, which still bore last-minute corrections made in pencil. Thirty-eight minutes later, the bill passed.

On the Sunday night following the vote, Roosevelt went on the radio to talk to the American public. This marked the first of what would become a regular feature of his presidency, a continuation of a custom he had begun while governor of New York. Roosevelt's informal radio speeches were called fireside chats because FDR wanted to give the impression that he was visiting with his listeners in their homes, talking directly to the people.

In a calm and clear voice, he told the public that night that the banking system would regain its health if they, the public, backed it. "I can assure you," he told millions of anxious listeners across the coun-try, "that it is safer to keep your money in a reopened bank than under the mattress."[22]

The move was a gamble, but it worked. Public confidence in the banking system returned immediately; on the first day after the holiday, deposits exceeded withdrawals. Within a month, 70 percent of banks nationwide had reopened. The quick response caused Roosevelt's adviser Raymond Moley to remark later that "capitalism was saved in eight days."[23]

The Brain Trust

The bank holiday was only a temporary measure that solved one specific problem. Much more work remained, and to carry it out Roosevelt drew upon the expertise of many people. In particular, three Columbia University professors, more than any other group or individual, helped FDR shape New Deal policy.

Roosevelt delivers one of his fireside chats to the nation. The informal talks rallied Americans' damaged morale.

Raymond Moley, Rexford Guy Tugwell, and Adolf A. Berle Jr. had advised FDR when he was both governor and presidential candidate. Because of their academic background, they became known as the Brains Trust, a term first used by *New York Times* reporter James Kieran. (Later the group was more often called the Brain Trust because the singular form was easier to say; both terms sometimes also referred to any high officials of the New Deal.)

Raymond Moley, a professor of government and public law, was plainspoken and blunt. When he encountered people he considered incompetent, he dismissed them as "cookie pushers." His theories stressed the need for immediate, large-scale

Economist Rexford G. Tugwell became part of Roosevelt's Brain Trust because of his expertise in agricultural and farm issues.

efforts by the government, particularly relief and public works programs, social security, and unemployment insurance.

Rexford G. Tugwell, a young economist, was part of the group because of his expertise in agriculture and farm issues. A brilliant thinker and speaker, Tugwell's main contribution was the development of a farm program that relied on long-term planning and production control.

The group's third member was law professor and economic specialist Adolf A. Berle Jr. Berle, a prodigy who had graduated from Harvard Law School at twenty-one, stressed the importance of helping individual families—for example, by means of programs to support home and farm mortgages.

The Brain Trust members shared some common attitudes. They agreed that it was the duty of the government to supply relief directly to citizens, rather than letting it "trickle down" as Hoover had done. They felt that cooperation between government and business was crucial. The government should lend businesses money; businesses, in turn, should allow stricter regulations. Stricter regulation, the Brain Trust argued, might have prevented the stock market crash in the first place.

The opinions of the three could also vary widely. This led to lively discussions and occasional arguments. The variety of opinion suited FDR, since he was always looking for new paths and untried methods.

Typically, the trio would supply the president with a wide range of approaches for dealing with a given problem. FDR would consider each one, then pick and choose from among them. This problem-solving strategy led to the use of a variety of approaches, and it also encouraged healthy rivalries among the advisers. Abe

Wilted Advisers

In Franklin D. Roosevelt: A Rendezvous with Destiny, *Raymond Moley recalls Roosevelt's learning curve. The technique remained the same after he became president.*

"The Governor was at once a student, a cross-examiner, and a judge. He would listen with rapt attention for a few minutes and then break in with a question whose sharpness was characteristically blurred with an anecdotal introduction or an air of sympathetic agreement with the speaker. . . . The questions . . . would become meatier, more informed—the infallible index to the amount [Roosevelt] was picking up in the evening's course. By midnight . . . the visitor . . . would look a trifle wilted; and the Governor . . . would be making vigorous pronouncements on the subject we had been discussing, waving his cigarette holder to emphasize his points."

Fortas, a young lawyer in Roosevelt's administration who later became a Supreme Court justice, once remarked that FDR was like symphony conductor Arturo Toscanini in the way he handled these multiple voices:

> Roosevelt was a master at controlling friction and making it constructive.... He knew how to conduct an orchestra and when to favor the first fiddles and when to favor the trombones. He knew how to employ and manipulate people.[24]

Other Advisers

Roosevelt relied on the Brain Trust for broad policy advice, but for the day-to-day operations in the early years, he relied on tough veteran politicians and aides. Among these were FDR's longtime personal aide, Louis Howe, and Democratic national chairman James A. Farley.

Among those who also had the president's ear were cabinet members, including Labor Secretary Frances Perkins, the first woman to be appointed to a cabinet-level position, and bright young lawyers like Thomas Corcoran and Ben Cohen, who did much of the nuts-and-bolts work of assembling New Deal policy.

As time went on, Eleanor Roosevelt also became a prominent figure in high-level decision making. This was a sharp change from the retiring roles most previous First Ladies had played. More and more, Mrs. Roosevelt's opinions were a strong element in her husband's policy decisions. Her unwavering commitment to fair treatment for minorities and women had particular influence.

Eleanor Roosevelt also served as her wheelchair-bound husband's eyes and

First Lady Eleanor Roosevelt played an active role in her husband's administration. Eleanor not only gathered firsthand information for her husband, but she also took on several pet political projects herself.

ears by taking extensive trips in search of information about the state of the nation. Her travels across America became so frequent, in fact, that it was a rarity when she stayed home. In 1935 a headline in the Washington *Star* half-jokingly announced: "MRS. ROOSEVELT SPENDS NIGHT AT WHITE HOUSE."[25]

Quick Legislation

In normal times, Congress and the executive office (the president and his staff) are often at odds with each other. This tension is an example of the system of checks and balances that is an important part of American political life, designed to keep any

one part of the government from becoming too powerful. Because of this system, Congress does not have to pass laws that the president requests. The president, in turn, can veto laws passed during his administration, but a large congressional majority can override a veto. The Supreme Court, as the third balancing element, reviews cases arising from disagreements over laws or treaties.

But the spring of 1933 was not a normal time. The popular demand for immediate, decisive action that had rocketed Roosevelt into office also swept aside the opposing influence of Republicans and conservative Democrats in the House and Senate. These bodies rallied behind FDR perhaps more than any Congress has ever supported any other president.

For a short time, FDR enjoyed extraordinary authority in shaping national policy. Many experts feel that his power was as great as that of Lincoln in the early days of the Civil War, when unprecedented executive actions were taken to try to preserve the Union. "The depression crisis was not of the magnitude of the secession crisis," according to Frank Freidel, "but the entire nation was unified behind Roosevelt as passionately as the northern half had been . . . behind Lincoln." [26]

This authority led to occasional cries of "dictator" from those who feared Roosevelt had too much power. (In later years, Adolf Berle would tease FDR by beginning his letters and memos, "Dear Caesar.") Most lawmakers agreed, however, that the only way change could happen quickly would be to focus authority on the executive office.

FDR was aware that the support would not last. The so-called honeymoon period he enjoyed with Congress would end soon. He moved swiftly and established as many of his programs as possible in a short amount of time. The immediacy of his actions won many loyal followers who reveled in the promised changes even though the results were still forthcoming. As Raymond Moley remarked to Frances Perkins as they watched Roosevelt being sworn in

A Charmer

These memories of New Deal staffer James H. Rowe Jr., reprinted in Katie Loucheim's anthology The Making of the New Deal, *illustrate Roosevelt's ease with people and smooth political manipulation.*

"That complete charm was always there. I remember the first time I met him. . . . The President looked up. I can still remember this as though it happened yesterday. He said, 'Jim, I knew you were here and all week I've been wanting to get you in because I want to ask you about two or three real problems I've got and I want your advice. And I'll get to them.' It took me two days to realize he didn't mean it. He did that with everyone all the time.

[New Deal lawyer] Tommy Corcoran made a point about him once, and I think it's probably valid. I asked, 'Why is it FDR's so good?' Tommy said, 'Look, there you are. You have to work for a living. Here I am. I have to work for a living. This fellow had nothing to do all his life except politics. He's spent the bulk of his life in politics. He got to know every wrinkle of politics. He got to know how to handle anybody, and he worked at it 100 percent. You work at it 5 percent, and I work at it 7.'"

as president, "Well, he's taken the ship of state and turned it right around."[27]

A Flurry of Bills

Roosevelt's swift assumption of the "helm" of the ship of state resulted in a three-month flurry of activity that newspapers dubbed the Hundred Days. During this period, mid-March to mid-June 1933, Congress passed more recovery, relief, and reform legislation than at any other time in American history.

In all, fifteen major laws and a host of smaller ones were passed during the Hundred Days. Among the most significant were the National Industrial Recovery Act, the Civilian Conservation Corps Act, the Federal Emergency Relief Act, the Agricultural Adjustment Act, the Tennessee Valley Authority Act, the Securities Act, and the Home Owners Refinancing Act. One minor but highly popular bill legalized the sale of wine and weak beer, thus paving the way for the repeal of the Eighteenth Amendment, the Prohibition law that had criminalized the manufacture and sale of alcohol in America.

It seemed to some observers that the rapid-fire legislation of the Hundred Days was haphazard, and critics accused FDR and Congress of making up the New Deal as they went along. In part, the inconsistencies and seemingly contradictory policies FDR put forward reflected his pragmatic approach to politics. His controversial pro-

While a radio plays in the background, a farmer reads the depression-era newspaper Wallaces' Farmer. *Although radio was a new medium when FDR took office, the innovative president capitalized on the medium's ability to speak directly to the nation.*

The Angel Gabriel

Many people who knew FDR were amazed at his transformation during the Hundred Days. In quotes reprinted in The Great Depression, *Robert McElvaine illustrates this change.*

"'Many of us who have known him long and well,' wrote *Nation* editor Ernest Gruening in May 1933, 'ask ourselves if this is the same man.' 'Was I just fooled before the election,' wondered Republican [newspaper] editor William Allen White, 'or has he developed? . . . I have never had to eat my words before.' [Someone] who had worked with Roosevelt in the Wilson days insisted, 'that fellow in there is not the fellow we used to know. There's been a miracle here.' Herbert Feis described the public perception of that miracle: 'The outside public seems to believe as if Angel Gabriel had come to earth.'"

grams needed to satisfy many different interest groups and schools of thought. Roosevelt, skilled in the art of pleasing opposing sides, felt that an occasionally messy or incomplete compromise was the price of getting things done.

FDR won on some points and lost on others with Congress; he made many friends and many enemies. Overall, however, the executive and legislative branches worked together during the Hundred Days with a rare smoothness. As Frank Freidel writes, "Congress contributed much, both negatively and positively, and the legislation of the spring of 1933 is a monument to it as well as to Roosevelt."[28]

Using the Media

Roosevelt has often been called the first great American radio voice. Radio was in its infancy when FDR first took public office, and by the time he became president, he was able to make full use of the medium. His fireside chats were immensely popular; people dropped everything to listen to them. Those who didn't have radio sets visited friends or neighbors who did, or they gathered to hear the broadcasts in appliance shops.

Roosevelt used the chats to soothe his audience's fears, lift their spirits, and explain the issues of the day. FDR was not an intellectual, but he had a gift for explaining complex theories and situations in ways that everyone could understand. Retired Supreme Court justice Oliver Wendell Holmes remarked after talking with Roosevelt in 1933 that the president had "a second-class intellect, but a first-class temperament."[29]

In addition to his radio talks, Roosevelt shrewdly used the news media in other ways. For instance, he timed his press conferences to keep up pressure on Congress regarding bills he wanted to push. Even his manner of holding news conferences, a radical change from that of the previous president, helped cement his perceptive use of the media.

Herbert Hoover had always been a remote figure to reporters. Most communication that journalists had with the White House during his administration was through spokesmen. By contrast, FDR began an open-door policy for reporters and instigated a revolutionary new concept: the friendly press conference.

He allowed reporters to crowd into the Oval Office twice a week, joking with them, asking their opinions, and making them feel like insiders. This led to generally en-thusiastic coverage in the newspapers, which in turn bolstered the president's support among voters and ultimately in Congress. The net effect was to pull more and more people into the Roosevelt camp. As William Leuchtenberg notes, almost everyone—even Republicans—gathered around the president:

> The opposition press suspended criticism of the President; corporations, labor unions, and farm organizations pledged their cooperation; and GOP leaders urged the country to rally around the Democratic chief executive. Alf Landon [the governor of Kansas who would later run against

Roosevelt holds a press conference at his summer home in August 1939. The press conferences were part of FDR's open-door policy.

"This Great Army"

From the beginning, Roosevelt saw the battle against the depression in military terms. These words, reprinted in Looking Forward, *one of FDR's books of papers and essays, are from his inaugural address in 1933.*

"If we are to go forward, we must move as a trained and loyal army willing to sacrifice for the good of a common discipline. . . . We are, I know, ready and willing to submit our lives and property to such discipline, because it makes possible a leadership which aims at a larger good. . . . I assume unhesitatingly the leadership of this great army of our people dedicated to a disciplined attack upon our common problems. . . .

For the trust reposed in me I will return the courage and the devotion that befit the time. I can do no less. . . .

The people of the United States have not failed. In their need they have registered a mandate that they want direct, vigorous action. They have asked for discipline and direction under leadership. They have made me the present instrument of their wishes. In the spirit of the gift, I take it."

FDR in 1936] declared: "If there is any way in which a member of that species thought to be extinct, a Republican Governor of a mid-western state, can aid [the President] in the fight, I now enlist for the duration of the war."[30]

The Mood in Washington

As the Hundred Days came to a close in the summer of 1933, Roosevelt faced the task of putting into practice his daunting array of new laws.

He was helped by the thousands of people flocking to Washington to be part of the exciting new developments in government. New agencies were being created daily, and new recruits—many of them young, ambitious, and idealistic—were arriving to carry them out.

Lady Bird Johnson—along with her husband, future president Lyndon Johnson—was among the bright young people who came to Washington during the early New Deal days. She later recalled of those years:

It was a yeasty, exciting time. The lights burned long in those offices, and the people really felt that they could roll up their sleeves and make America great. Lyndon had an expression about that: "You feel like charging Hell with a bucket of water." This feeling, this enthusiasm, pushed them a long ways. There were very few times in our country's life when so many good minds gathered together in that city intent on raising the level of living and the safety of the American people.[31]

The sleepy old southern city fairly buzzed with activity. Even veteran politicians and journalists felt the excitement. The atmosphere in Washington, veteran newsman Arthur Krock wrote at the time, was "distinctly hopeful":

[Washington] welcomes the "new deal," even though it is not sure what the new deal is going to be. It is ready to be enthusiastic over any display of leadership, any outline of a reconstruction program. Not for years. . . has a new President been more likely to gain gratitude and praise. . . for the simple fact of being able to achieve any program at all.[32]

Everyone was curious to see what would happen next, when the new programs went into effect. Most people, however, were optimistic that there had been any action at all. Humorist Will Rogers captured the attitude of many toward the country's vigorous leader when he remarked, "If he burned down the capitol, we would cheer and say, 'Well, we at least got a fire started anyhow.'"[33] But now it was time to turn the strong talk and new legislation into reality.

3 Programs for Farming and Industry

The country needs and, unless I mistake its temper, the country demands bold, persistent experimentation. It is common sense to take a method and try it: If it fails, admit it frankly and try another. But above all, try something.

Franklin D. Roosevelt

The bank holiday had brightened the economic picture, but the improvement was temporary and shaky. The legislation of the Hundred Days promised more lasting relief.

The Alphabet Administration

Roosevelt felt that four interrelated components were crucial to success. One was reform to help farmers regain prosperity. Another was similar aid to industry. A third was direct relief—that is, jobs and financial assistance for people who were unemployed and needy. The fourth aspect of Roosevelt's basic philosophy lay in revising America's economic policies—that is, laws controlling financial institutions and issues.

Each law passed during the Hundred Days created new agencies aimed at reaching one or more of these goals. Each agency had a title and an acronym, an abbreviation made of letters. The bewildering array of new organizations and titles pouring out of Washington in 1933 provided a nickname for the new government: the Alphabet Administration.

Most of these programs, Roosevelt hoped, would be temporary and limited. He believed that short-term solutions would be enough to bring slow, steady recovery. "We are a little bit like the old railroad train that has to travel up a long grade," he told reporters. "We have got the train started and it is running, let us say, twenty miles an hour. We must get that train to go forty miles an hour and then there is an assurance that it will go over the top."[34]

Saving the Farms

A healthy farmland was, in Roosevelt's view, perhaps the single most important element in creating a recovery. Roosevelt and his key advisers believed that the New Deal would succeed or fail on the success of its farm program.

The situation in America's agricultural heartland was grim. Farms both large and small were collapsing. The total farm income for the nation in 1932 was less than

The Farm Problem

"Fifty million men, women and children immediately within our borders are directly concerned with the present and the future of agriculture. Another fifty or sixty million people who are engaged in business and industry . . . are at last coming to understand the simple fact that their lives and their futures are also profoundly concerned with the prosperity of agriculture. They realize more and more that there will be no outlet for their products unless their fifty million fellow Americans who are directly concerned with agriculture are given the buying power to buy city products.

Our economic life today is a seamless web. Whatever our vocation, we are forced to recognize that while we have enough factories and enough machines in the United States to supply all our needs, these factories will be closed part of the time and the machines will lie idle if the buying power of fifty million people remains restricted or dead."

FDR visits with a farmer who is receiving drought relief in 1936. Roosevelt gained a reputation for caring about the average American.

State highway officials oversee the eviction of sharecroppers in Missouri. Unable to sell their crops, farmers suffered greatly during the depression.

one-third of what it had been for 1929— and 1929 had been a bad year for farmers.

Prices for farm products were at rock-bottom lows. Farmers were still growing crops, but they were unable to make a profit on what they grew and often could not sell their goods at all. Some midwesterners were forced to burn their corn and wheat crops just to keep warm; it was cheaper than burning coal. One midwestern farmer recalls:

A county just east of here, they burned corn in their courthouse all winter. . . . In South Dakota, the county elevator listed corn as minus three cents. *Minus* three cents a bushel. If you wanted to sell 'em a bushel of corn, you had to bring in three cents.[35]

The inability to sell crops, coupled with widespread poverty, led to a strange situation. All across the country, people were going hungry while huge quantities of food rotted in warehouses. Tons of food and millions of gallons of milk, among other products, were dumped by roadsides because no one could sell them.

Roosevelt responded with characteristic boldness by suggesting several new, untested, and sometimes drastic ways to reform farm legislation. These new policies operated under an umbrella organization, the Agricultural Adjustment Administration (AAA).

In a sense, the theory behind the AAA's activities was the reverse of Hoover's trickle-down philosophy. If farm prices rose and farmers could get other breaks in their finances, Roosevelt reasoned, farmers would again have money and their buying power would help other areas of the marketplace. The whole economy would benefit from money "trickling up."

Some of the measures the AAA handled were fairly conservative and low key, such as the Emergency Farm Mortgage Act, which provided low-interest mortgages to farmers. Others, such as the Agricultural Adjustment bill, proved to be controversial.

Not Raising Crops or Animals

The Agricultural Adjustment bill was designed to boost farm prices with a program called a domestic allotment or farm subsidy plan. Under plans like this one, production is limited because farmers are paid *not* to produce certain crops or raise animals. In the program's early days, they were also paid to destroy existing crops and animals; for example, ten million acres of cotton were plowed under and six million piglets were slaughtered.

Roosevelt reasoned that fewer farm products would create a scarcity of those products, and they would be in greater demand. This greater demand would drive their prices upward. Farmers could then afford to sell their goods at a reasonable profit.

The program fit poorly with FDR's overall scheme of creating an economy where goods and services would be abundant. However, he and his main agricultural advisers—Secretary of Agriculture Henry A. Wallace and Rexford Tugwell, now an assistant secretary of agriculture—felt it was a necessary first step.

To some economists today, the farm subsidy plan seems relatively cautious. The system is even still in place to a degree. In

FDR signs his farm bill into law. The bill provided incentives for farmers not to produce as many crops.

1933, however, many considered it extreme, illogical, even crazy.

Politicians and citizens alike had a hard time understanding the program. The plan's backers admitted that the farm subsidy plan was not perfect, but they argued that the alternative was equally unacceptable: a country full of farmers who grew crops and raised animals that no one could buy. Robert McElvaine writes:

> What sense did it make to destroy food in a nation where millions were hungry and a world where hundreds of millions were starving? Very little perhaps, but no less than it did to have such poverty and want in the midst of abundance and unused capacity in the first place.[36]

During Roosevelt's first years, the plan worked to a degree. Crop prices climbed sharply and rural debt fell dramatically. Overall farm income rose by 50 percent. As Roosevelt had hoped, farmers then began to make purchases from merchants and mail-order houses, so other parts of the economy also benefited.

Rising costs for farm equipment, however, eliminated some of the gains. Also, a series of severe droughts, not the AAA, created some of the scarcity that drove up prices. And many farmers who took money to not produce on certain acreage raised crops extra-efficiently on the remaining

Migrant workers carry their meager belongings from farm to farm as they search for work.

An editorial cartoon endorses FDR's National Recovery Administration (NRA), arguing that it provides a bridge between the government, employer, and employee.

acreage, a practice that cost the government money and undermined overall recovery.

The result was that the farm bill did not result in widespread recovery for agriculture. Not until 1941 did annual farm income exceed that of 1929. Most historians today regard the subsidy program as a partial success, neither a disaster nor a great achievement. However, one farmer from Iowa puts a more positive spin on the situation: "It was Wallace [the secretary of agriculture] who saved us, put us back on our feet. He understood our problems."[37]

The Blue Eagle Rises

As he addressed the farm problem, Roosevelt also turned his attention to reviving industry.

When FDR took office, about half of America's factories had closed, and its once mighty production capacity was almost unused. There was little money to buy raw materials, pay workers, or invest in maintenance and new equipment. The key to recovery, FDR felt, was careful planning that would eliminate waste and regulate such areas as prices, working conditions, and wages. The stock market crash of 1929 had occurred in a business environment that had few controls. Roosevelt believed that government regulation was necessary to revive and support American industry's dismal prospects.

He therefore persuaded Congress to pass the National Industrial Recovery Act, which gave him authority to establish the National Recovery Administration (NRA). This agency was designed to create codes that would standardize certain industrial practices, practices that had been unregulated for too long. According to Robert McElvaine, the NRA "amounted to an admission that the 'unfettered [unchained] marketplace' was no longer a viable means of governing the national economy."[38]

Roosevelt wanted the NRA to be a cooperative effort between business, labor, and government. He often referred to it as a "partnership in planning." He made membership voluntary because he did not want to antagonize workers or business leaders. But he also tried to make it appealing. Businesses that agreed to participate would receive various benefits, such as government help in preventing competitive price cutting. Labor, meanwhile, was promised presidential support on important issues such as minimum wages, child labor, and contract negotiations.

Meanwhile, the New Dealers sought to convince the public that buying from NRA businesses was patriotic. Merchants proudly advertised their membership to customers with posters of the organization's symbol, a blue eagle, above the slogan "We Do Our Part." Massive public-relations stunts, such as a parade of 250,000 people marching down New York's Fifth Avenue, drove the message home.

General Hugh S. Johnson was Roosevelt's choice to head the NRA. The peppery, plainspoken, hard-drinking Johnson had few illusions about the difficulties involved in satisfying opposing factions. When asked by reporters what he expected from his new job, he remarked, "It will be red fire at first and dead cats afterwards."[39]

Johnson was a whirlwind of activity during the NRA's first year. He and his

---

"Now You Do Something"

Shortly after Roosevelt's inauguration, William E. Leuchtenberg reports in Franklin D. Roosevelt and the New Deal, *the gloom that had settled on America began to lift, as the president's message of hope and confidence began to spread.*

"Two weeks after Roosevelt took office, the country seemed a changed place. Where once there had been apathy and despondency, there was now an immense sense of movement. If the country did not know in what direction it was moving, it had great expectations; the spell of lassitude [fatigue] had been snapped. On the walls of Thomas A. Edison, Inc., in West Orange, New Jersey, President Charles Edison posted a notice:

'President Roosevelt has done his part: now you do something. Buy something—buy anything, anywhere; paint your kitchen, send a telegram, give a party, get a car, pay a bill, rent a flat, fix your roof, get a haircut, see a show, build a house, take a trip, sing a song, get married. It does not matter what you do—but get going and keep going. This old world is starting to move.'"

An elderly man and child pick grapes, filling a barrel that announces their participation in the NRA program.

staff crisscrossed the country, helping create codes for industries and talking to business leaders. On one occasion, he marched into the White House and handed Roosevelt three separate codes to approve. As the president was signing the last one, Johnson grabbed the papers and raced to catch a plane for the next destination. The president, perhaps making a veiled reference to the alcohol problems that would later bring Johnson's career to a halt, half jokingly told reporters, "He hasn't been seen since."[40]

In all, 541 codes standardizing various sectors of industry were passed. Unfortunately, the codes did not work well. Partly this was because NRA membership was voluntary, so government could do nothing to enforce the new rules. Also, the largest businesses within a given industry were allowed great power in creating codes for their sectors—a classic case, critics charged, of the fox guarding the henhouse.

The Blue Eagle Falters

Even for well-meaning members, compliance with the codes was difficult. The standards had to cover a vast array of situations and satisfy many conflicting groups; the results satisfied virtually no one. Rather than a few clearly written, all-encompassing codes, the NRA regulations were a bewildering tangle of codes that tried to cover every situation in every business from steel factories to the feather-duster industry.

Johnson successfully convinced several major industries to join up, including ship-building, electrical manufacturers, lumber, soft coal, and steel. Not all of America's business leaders were sold, however. One leading industrialist, Henry Ford, thought the agency was a conspiracy cooked up by international bankers and his competitors. He said of the NRA's blue eagle logo, "I wouldn't put that Roosevelt buzzard on my cars."[41]

The NRA also failed from the viewpoint of workers. Leaders of organized labor unions complained that the codes did not go far enough in regulating hours, wages, and other issues of importance to employees. "In the face of such criticism," historian Ellis W. Hawley writes of the NRA, "the system was in an almost constant state of turmoil and reorganization."[42]

As the criticism mounted during the agency's first year, Johnson himself became increasingly unstable. His enormous bursts of energy were followed by equally massive drinking binges, and he began disappearing for days at a time. In Sep-tember 1934 Roosevelt replaced the fiery but unpredictable general with an oversight group, the National Industrial Recovery Board.

Although most of the NRA's goals were never met, it did succeed to a degree. It set the stage for future laws governing such issues as contract negotiation and minimum wage. Perhaps more importantly, it boosted the nation's optimism and confidence in business, by emphasizing the need for ethical practices and the advantages of working cooperatively. Ellis W. Hawley summarizes:

> Historians have generally regarded the NRA's code system as one of the New Deal's greatest failures. . . . Some, however, have credited the program with giving an initial psychological lift to the nation's depressed spirits, helping to improve business ethics, putting an end to child labor, and paving the way for mass unionization.[43]

Relief for the nation's farmers and businesspeople was only part of Roosevelt's New Deal strategy. Another major aspect of his plan was designed to put money directly into the pockets of the American citizens who were suffering the most, in the form of relief payments and works projects.

4 Programs for Relief, Works Projects, and More

Better the occasional faults of a Government that lives in a spirit of charity than the constant omission of a Government frozen in the ice of its own indifference.

Franklin D. Roosevelt

As his plans to revive agriculture and business moved forward, FDR also turned his attention to another problem: directly relieving the suffering of those Americans—at least thirty million people—who had no regular income.

Private charity had risen to its highest level in history, and local government spending for welfare had doubled from the previous decade. Millions of families, however, still stubbornly and proudly refused to accept any kind of charity.

Instead, they doubled up households and economized in other ways. A researcher surveying laid-off workers reported:

> Whole families combine in a sort of super-family, so that one rent will do instead of two. Relatives of all degrees gather round an income like flies round a honey-pot—anyone who has an income will find himself swamped either with appeals for help or with non-paying guests.[44]

Roosevelt had long been a supporter of direct government assistance, or relief,

as an answer to this problem. Since his days as governor of New York, he had viewed relief as both a practical necessity and a humanitarian duty. "In broad terms," he had stated as governor in 1931, "I assert that modern society, acting through its government, owes the definite obligation to prevent the starvation or the

Unemployed men obtain a meal at a soup kitchen. Such kitchens were run by private charities.

Harry Hopkins was the head of FERA, the Federal Emergency Relief Administration. Hopkins was so influential that reporters called him the assistant president.

istrator, and a longtime Roosevelt colleague. In time he became so closely associated with Roosevelt and the New Deal, in fact, that reporters began calling him the assistant president.

Hopkins had a reputation for speedy decision making, and his plan for FERA involved typically quick behavior. He thought the best solution was to spend money rapidly so it could disperse into the economy. His spending plan worked to a remarkable degree: during his first two hours as federal relief administrator, Hopkins spent $5 million. Raymond Moley later remarked that Hopkins had "a capacity for quick and, it should be added, expensive action."[46]

dire want of any of its fellow men and women who try to maintain themselves but cannot."[45]

Jobs for the Unemployed

As president, Roosevelt's answer to the problem was the Federal Emergency Relief Administration (FERA). This agency gave states large grants that were passed on as direct cash payments for needy families. It also evolved into a program for creating work relief, that is, projects that provided jobs for the unemployed.

Roosevelt chose Harry Hopkins to head FERA. Hopkins was an informal and likable individual, a highly capable admin-

The CWA

FERA's direct cash payments to people who could not hold jobs, such as the severely disabled and mothers with young children, would continue into 1936. The agency's main focus, however, quickly shifted to works projects. This was because Roosevelt and Hopkins realized that the existing system would not be enough to see people through the coming winter of 1933–34, which looked like it was going to be an especially fierce one. The president wanted to provide jobs to put money into people's hands, knowing that they would require fuel and warm clothing in addition to food and shelter.

A subagency, the Civil Works Administration (CWA), was formed in the fall of 1933 as a temporary measure. It was temporary because FDR was not eager to establish a permanent works project administration; he believed that recovery was

In 1936 Harry Hopkins, FDR's ally in creating his welfare programs, made these spirited remarks, which have been reprinted in The FDR Years: On Roosevelt and His Legacy.

"I am getting sick and tired of these people on the WPA and local relief rolls being called chiselers and cheats. . . . These people . . . are just like the rest of us. They don't drink any more than the rest of us, they don't lie any more, they're no lazier than the rest of us—they're pretty much a cross-section of the American people. . . .

I have gone all over the [arguments favored by conservatives] that people are poor because they are bad. I don't believe it."

coming soon. As he told his advisers, "We must not take the position that we are going to have permanent depression in this country."[47]

The CWA provided work for up to four million people at a given time. The variety of jobs was wide, including construction work, literacy teaching, and white-collar jobs in such areas as medicine and social work. CWA employees built some 240,000 miles of roads and 5,000 new public buildings, built or improved over 800 small airports, and laid thousands of miles of sewer lines and storm-drainage systems.

The CWA poured a billion dollars into the economy within a few months of its formation. Employees received weekly paychecks of fifteen dollars, which maintained minimum living standards for an estimated twelve million people. Even then, fifteen dollars was not much—but it was two and a half times the typical FERA payment, and it allowed most families to survive.

Roosevelt and Hopkins preferred this system of providing jobs rather than straight cash payments. Working in exchange for a paycheck "preserves a man's morale," Hopkins remarked. "It saves his skill. It gives him a chance to do something socially useful." CWA employees generally felt the same; working kept their pride intact. CWA field investigator Lorena Hickok interviewed a middle-aged former salesman who said the day he received his CWA identification card was "the biggest day in my whole life. At last I could say, 'I've got a job.'"[48]

Dams, Roadways, and Bridges

As a short-term solution, the CWA was adequate. As the depression dragged on, however, some New Dealers argued that a larger works project program was needed for full recovery.

At first Roosevelt balked because he still felt recovery would come soon. He also argued that the proposed program would cost too much. One of his biggest aims was to balance the budget, and he was reluctant to start expensive projects that would jeopardize that goal. Gradually he came to believe that a larger project was needed, however, and he sped up formation of the more ambitious Public Works Administration (PWA).

The PWA operated with a budget that was small compared to its ambitious set of projects: about $3 billion for jobs and related spending-stimulus programs and about $6 billion for construction projects. In part, this was a reflection of Roosevelt's conservative attitude toward spending. He wanted to fund only projects that would eventually earn back their cost.

Emphasizing this conservative view, Roosevelt appointed as PWA director a man who represented the opposite end of the scale from the free-spending Harry Hopkins. Interior Secretary Harold Ickes was a serious-minded man with a reputation for hating to spend money, as well as a

reputation for absolute incorruptibility; reporters dubbed him "Honest Harold." When Frances Perkins first suggested Ickes to Roosevelt, she commented, "I have been very well impressed with his kind of punctilious [painstaking], fussy scrutiny of detail. . . . That's exactly what you want, I think, in a public works administrator."[49]

For the most part, Ickes and his colleagues succeeded. Ickes inspired responsible behavior at all levels of the agency, and the PWA established a strong reputation for good management. The agency's extremely cautious approach, however, led critics to complain that the PWA was too slow moving in approving and administering new projects.

Between 1933 and 1939, over a million men were employed and over thirty-five thousand separate projects were completed by the PWA. As a result, the total volume of new construction in the nation more than doubled. Every county in the United States except for three was the recipient of at

An unemployed man sits outside a store. FDR's Public Works Administration (PWA) put many unemployed people back to work.

Harold Ickes, director of the PWA, garnered respect for his serious management style but also criticism for moving too cautiously.

least one PWA project; these included the building or repair of highways, sewage systems, bridges, lighthouses, dams, hospitals, low-cost housing, airports, and warships. Many of the agency's creations are still in use today and are among America's best-known monuments.

Losing a Generation

According to historian John Salmond, by 1934 roughly one-third of all sixteen- to twenty-four-year-olds in America's labor pool were unemployed, drifting around the country in search of work. Many more young people were joining the ranks daily, dropping out of school to support their families however they could. An entire generation was in danger of growing up unskilled, untrained, and lacking self-confidence. Eleanor Roosevelt remarked, "I have moments of real terror when I think we might be losing this generation."[50]

The CCC

One of the best-known and most popular of the New Deal programs, the Civilian Conservation Corps (CCC), employed these young men in national parks and wildernesses. The CCC was a particular favorite of Roosevelt's since it combined two of his greatest interests: preservation of America's forest lands and jobs for America.

Roosevelt had grown up with a strong sense of responsibility to land conservation, and the agency, he felt, formed a direct link between two things necessary for a nation's survival: the vigor of its workers and the strength of its land. "The CCC," writes historian Page Smith, "combined Roosevelt's passion for reforestation with his and Eleanor's concern for young people, especially for unemployed youth."[51]

Unmarried men between the ages of eighteen and twenty-five could join the CCC for up to two years. Recruits were assigned to camps and given room, board, and thirty dollars every month, twenty-five of which went directly home to their families. At the agency's peak, more than half a million men were stationed in about 2,500 camps. In all, over three million men passed through the CCC.

In exchange, they performed work such as erosion and flood control, wildlife protection, disaster and fire relief, construction of shelters, and restoration of historical sites. The agency's single greatest achievement, however, was its massive reseeding and maintenance of forestland. According to John Salmond, three-quarters of all the trees planted in the United States before World War II were planted in less than a decade by the CCC.

The CCC was immediately popular among lawmakers and the public as well as its employees, for several reasons besides the obvious one of steady work. Its value was easily seen; even FDR's political enemies approved of preservation. Also, camps were usually near small towns that enjoyed economic boosts from serving the employees stationed there. Finally, the public saw CCC camps as safe environments where vigorous, disciplined outdoor labor was encouraged.

Discrimination

The CCC has been faulted for its poor civil rights record, since its camps were segregated along racial lines and there were recurring charges of discrimination against blacks who applied for CCC positions. Women, moreover, were not eligible at all. These conditions, which run counter to today's standards of equal rights and opportunity, may have reflected the influence of the program's director, Robert Fechner, a conservative, southern-born labor leader. Indeed, FDR alleged throughout his presidency that he could not do more for black people because he could not afford to alienate conservative southern politicians.

Despite its faults, however, the CCC was overall a great success. As Frank Freidel writes, "The CCC . . . was the most widely praised of the New Deal programs. Roosevelt took justified personal pride in it."[52]

A related agency, the National Youth Administration (NYA), gave young men (and women) the chance to work close to their homes. It provided millions of grants that allowed young people to stay in high school and college while working part-time and during the summer. It also trained them in specific skills and helped them find work when the training was complete.

A poster encourages young men to find jobs with the Civilian Conservation Corps (CCC), one of the most popular New Deal programs.

Young men of the CCC thin a stand of Scotch pine in a national forest.

The TVA

In 1933, New Deal surveys estimated, nine out of ten American farms had no electricity. They relied instead on gasoline engines, hand labor, and animal power. Kerosene lanterns were predominantly used for light, and wood or coal for cooking and heating.

The Tennessee Valley Authority (TVA) was the first of an ambitious series of programs designed to change this situation by bringing cheap, plentiful electricity to rural America. Like the CCC, the TVA was a popular program that sought to combine massive public works projects with improvements to the land.

It was also, like the CCC, one of the New Deal's greatest successes. Its complex of dams and power stations brought power to rural areas in seven states (Tennessee, Alabama, Mississippi, Kentucky, Virginia, North Carolina, and Georgia) along the Tennessee River. In doing so, it combined many of FDR's deepest concerns, such as planned land use, conservation of resources, cooperative effort, and the control of power utilities by the federal government instead of private interests. William E. Leuchtenberg writes:

> Roosevelt, with his long-standing interest in forest, land, and water, saw all of these elements as part of a whole. [The TVA] not merely unified development of the resources of the valley but [was]

a vast regional experiment in social planning which would affect directly the lives of the people of the valley.[53]

Much of the decision making was done by the people who lived in the affected communities. Although counter to the Brain Trust's tendency to centralize planning in the nation's capital, this unusual amount of local control was seen by many as a significant factor in the TVA's success.

In the early 1930s, however, critics charged that such intense cooperative regional planning was close to socialism, a form of government many of the farmers in the region opposed. As the project took shape, Roosevelt was asked how he planned to talk to people in the Tennessee River valley about this seeming paradox. Roosevelt replied, "I'll tell them it's neither fish nor fowl, but, whatever it is, it will taste awfully good to the people of the Tennessee Valley."[54]

The TVA, indeed, was very popular among the people on whom it had an immediate effect. Besides giving them cheap, reliable power to light their homes and power their equipment, the TVA also made the development of industry possible in one of the most severely depressed areas of the country. Furthermore, the agency sold fertilizer to local farmers, created projects that improved navigation on the river, helped control flooding in the region, and established reforestation and soil conservation programs.

The TVA was so successful that Roosevelt planned to create similar cooperative systems in other states, including Ohio and Washington. Those plans never materialized, but in the meantime the New Deal's Rural Electrification Administration (REA) encouraged farmers to form smaller cooperatives to create cheap power.

A Chance to Plan

When FDR submitted his proposal for a hydroelectric project in the Muscle Shoals region he emphasized the need for comprehensive planning. This extract is reprinted in Franklin D. Roosevelt: His Life and Times.

"It is clear that the Muscle Shoals development is but a small part of the potential public usefulness of the entire Tennessee River. Such use, if envisioned in its entirety, transcends [rises above] mere power development: it enters the wide fields of flood control, soil erosion, afforestation, elimination from agricultural use of marginal lands, and distribution and diversification of industry. In short, [it] leads logically to national planning for a complete river watershed involving many States and the future lives and welfare of millions. It touches and gives life to all forms of human concerns."

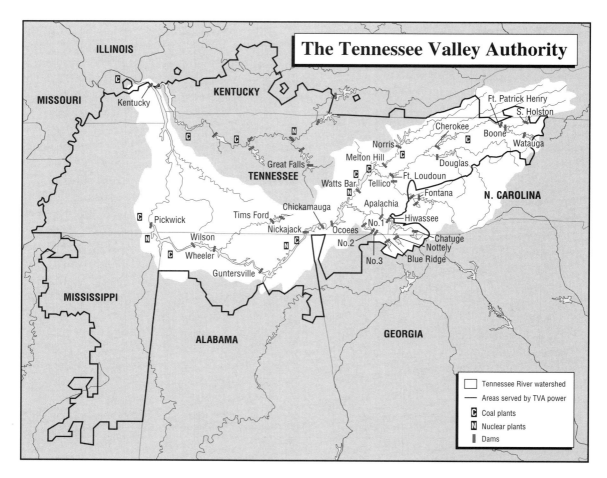

The Tennessee Valley Authority

By 1941, 40 percent of farms had electric power; by 1951 the percentage had increased to 90 percent. By the 1960s, Roosevelt's mission of the electrification of rural America was virtually complete. Furthermore, he successfully put the control of electrical power in the hands of the people who used it, not private companies. Historian John Muldowny summarizes the impact of farm electrification:

> The coming of electricity to rural America was one of the most important social and economic changes to occur during the New Deal era. . . . Running water, refrigeration, the radio, and better sanitation enabled farm families to experience many of the same comforts of life to which urban dwellers had long been accustomed. Electricity also improved farm technology and school and community life, it ended the toil and drudgery of farm life and lifted the spirits of farm families.[55]

Monetary Reform

Not all of the New Deal programs involved aid to industry or agriculture, direct relief, or putting people back to work. The fourth major part of FDR's overall plan was designed to restructure and strengthen the laws and policies governing America's financial systems.

Unlike many of the New Deal programs, Roosevelt saw these as permanent changes. He hoped they would help prevent future occurrences of devastating events such as the stock market crash. "Bailing out the banks in an emergency," Anthony Badger points out, "would be of little value if the faults in the system were not remedied at the same time."[56]

Trimming the national budget, a move in keeping with FDR's generally cautious financial philosophy, was one aspect of this reform. Roosevelt strongly believed that a balanced national budget was essential to a healthy economy. Even as he expanded public relief spending, FDR looked for ways to slash the budget. By persuading Congress and by issuing executive orders, he thus led moves to cut federal salaries, eliminate or consolidate agencies, and drastically reduce scientific research.

Another important permanent economic reform was the creation of the Federal Deposit Insurance Corporation (FDIC). This agency, which is now a vital part of the banking system, insures the safety of individual deposits. The initial amount that could be insured was $5,000; this has increased over the years with inflation, however, and currently stands at $100,000.

As a result of the new assurances made by the government, bank failures in America virtually disappeared after 1933. Individuals and families who deposited relatively small amounts in banks could rest easy, knowing that even if the bank failed, their deposits were safely insured. The devastating series of runs on banks ended quickly and has not returned.

The Securities Act

A third reform was the Securities Act, a measure that guarded against stock fraud

Crises

Elizabeth Wickenden of the Federal Emergency Relief Agency recalls here some of the more unusual crises she handled in the 1930s. The excerpt is from The Making of the New Deal.

"We had every kind of crisis you can imagine. We had a big fire in Lynchburg. We had a flood in the Florida Keys. We had a meningitis epidemic with people carrying the illness from one camp to another. But the funniest one was a telegram that came to my desk one day from the administrator in Vermont: 'The circus is stranded in some town in Vermont. This includes ten people, one elephant, many horses. Please advise.' We gave the people relief, but I can't remember what we did with the elephant."

by requiring that sellers provide more information about the stocks they were promoting. The Securities Act was the first piece of New Deal legislation to contend with the problems of unsafe speculation. Its sister bill, the Securities Exchange Act, had perhaps a more dramatic effect on shaping up the stock market. Though not passed until 1934, the Securities Exchange Act created the Securities and Exchange Commission (SEC), the first stock market regulatory agency. The SEC mandated that all stocks traded on the exchange market had to be licensed and registered by the commission. The SEC also banned the practice of selling large amounts of stock "on margin" (that is, on credit).

As the reforms and programs created in the Hundred Days became reality, Roosevelt expected the country to slowly but steadily recover. Much did change, but after two years the hoped-for widespread improvements had not arrived. This was almost certainly due in part to depressed economic conditions throughout the world.

FDR, meanwhile, was already beginning to face his second campaign for the presidency. Some of his programs did not appear to work well, and the failures were causing the president's popularity to slip. Roosevelt began rethinking some of his policies and programs, a process that began what many historians now call the Second New Deal.

5 A Second New Deal

There is a mysterious cycle in human events. To some generations much is given. Of other generations much is expected. This generation of Americans has a rendezvous with destiny.

Franklin D. Roosevelt, accepting the Democratic nomination for a second run at the presidency

Late 1934 through 1936 was a difficult period for the New Dealers. Things were better overall, but two years of hard work had still not put America back on track.

Recovery programs that had once seemed full of promise were not meeting proponents' expectations; the AAA and the NRA were particularly disappointing. About 20 percent of the nation's labor force was still unemployed. In addition, the Supreme Court issued a series of decisions that seriously undermined the infrastructure of the New Deal, by declaring some of its basic legislation unconstitutional.

Loss of Confidence

The president's popularity among voters dropped sharply, and there was reason to believe he might not be reelected in 1936 for a second term. FERA field investigator Martha Gellhorn noted this reversal of views among people she interviewed in 1934. People on relief or employed on works projects, once fiercely loyal to FDR, now were

> no longer sustained by confidence in the President. . . . They say to you, quietly, like people who have been betrayed but are too tired to be angry, "How does he expect us to live on that; does he know what food costs, what rents are, how can we keep clothes on the children?"[57]

Roosevelt's potential rivals had plenty of ammunition, and they continued their attacks on him. Democratic and Republican politicians who had once rallied behind the president began to move away from FDR's camp, and FDR no longer had nearly unanimous backing in Congress.

It was a tense time that required urgent action. Roosevelt and his advisers knew that if they lost the election, any chances of creating permanent reforms would almost certainly be gone. "Boys—this is our hour," Harry Hopkins told his staff. "We've got to get everything we want—a works program, social security, wages and hours, everything—now or never."[58]

Roosevelt began shifting his priorities to emphasize the New Deal's most popular

A cartoon criticizes FDR and his New Deal remedies for being unable to cure the patient—the American economy—though the president is successful in wooing a captivated Congress.

and effective programs. The most important new programs begun during this period included a new and massive public works agency, a system of social security, and a revised version of the flawed NRA to oversee reform of issues affecting business and labor. This period leading up to the 1936 election is often called the Second New Deal since it marked a move away from the sweeping changes of the Hundred Days toward a more moderate and long-term approach to reform.

Works Progress Administration

The public works project Roosevelt began during this time was a greatly expanded version of his earlier programs. The Works Progress Administration (WPA) was, in fact, the most extensive work relief agency in U.S. history.

In the three years of its existence, 1935 to 1938, it provided work for over five million people, injected more than $10 billion into the economy, and in total provided enough future work to employ thirteen million Americans. It was a huge program with a huge agenda, much of it controversial. Otis L. Graham points out that it aroused strong feelings both pro and con: "The WPA, according to polls, was most frequently named as the most popular single New Deal program, but also as the most unpopular!"[59]

The WPA's focus was on workers rather than business; it emphasized spending money on wages rather than machinery or materials. Its director, Harry Hopkins, stressed that projects should use human labor instead of mechanical power whenever possible, even though hiring large numbers of people was more expensive and less efficient.

Hopkins and Roosevelt also saw the WPA's emphasis on creating jobs as a way of maintaining morale by deemphasizing welfare payments. The president declared to Congress:

> Work must be found for able-bodied but destitute [penniless] workers. . . . We must preserve not only the bodies of the unemployed from destruction but also their self-respect, their self-reliance and courage and determination. [60]

The basic goals of the agency were similar to earlier works projects. Roosevelt told Congress that WPA projects would immediately create useful buildings or programs. Jobs would go to people already on relief rolls. Emphasis would be on training people or maintaining skills they already had. Projects that would stimulate the economy would get priority, so that WPA money could, as much as possible, circulate and return to the national treasury.

Finally, the WPA would not try to compete with private business. This meant that the pay scale for its employees had to be very low. Roosevelt did not want government work to be more attractive than private enterprise, and he wanted to encourage people to take better-paying jobs in private business whenever possible. As a result, WPA workers earned a monthly salary of only $60 to $100—barely half of what was then considered a minimum family budget.

Not Wholly Either, Something of Both

As the 1936 campaign picked up speed, Arthur Krock, a New York Times *columnist, illustrated the contrast between how Republicans and Democrats saw Roosevelt in a piece excerpted in* Franklin D. Roosevelt: A Rendezvous with Destiny *by Frank Freidel.*

"The Republicans say officially that the President is an impulsive, uninformed opportunist, lacking policy or stability, wasteful, reckless, unreliable in act and contract. . . . Mr. Roosevelt seeks to supervene [override] the constitutional processes of government, dominate Congress and the Supreme Court by illegal means and regiment the country. . . .

The Democrats say officially that the President is the greatest practical humanitarian who ever averted social upheaval, the wisest economic mechanician who ever modernized a government . . . savior and protector of the American way—including the capitalist system—and rebuilder of the nation. . . .

He is not wholly either, and he is certainly something of both. In the opinion of this writer he is much more of the latter than the former."

WPA workers improve a city's streets in this photograph from 1935. Many roads, buildings, parks, and other public structures built by the WPA are still in use today.

About three-quarters of the WPA's projects involved construction, and many of its creations are still in use. WPA workers improved 572,000 miles of rural roads, constructed 40,000 new buildings, and repaired 85,000 existing buildings. They built 78,000 new bridges and viaducts, 67,000 miles of city streets, and 24,000 miles of sidewalks. They created 8,000 parks, 3,700 recreation buildings, 350 airports, 1,500 athletic fields, 3,500 tennis courts, 440 swimming pools, 123 golf courses, and 28 miles of ski trails.

The WPA also sponsored a wide variety of nonconstruction projects. WPA workers stuffed mattresses, canned peaches, surveyed property boundaries, and sealed mines. They tended children, created books in Braille, counted cattle, and stitched winter coats.

Artists and Writers

Some of the WPA's best-known creations came from an agency that blended two of Roosevelt's strongly held beliefs. First, he felt that the basic WPA philosophy of making maximum use of an individual's skills should apply to creative people as much as to anyone else. It was foolish to put a concert violinist to work laying bricks, for instance, or make a sculptor dig ditches. Hopkins agreed; he once remarked of creative artists, "Hell, they've got to eat just like other people."[61]

At the same time, FDR believed that exposure to music, visual art, and the theater was an essential part of leading a well-balanced life. He encouraged the public to absorb culture whenever possible, even though, as Frank Freidel wryly notes, the president's personal measure of art lay in "whether or not the subject was a nautical one and, if so, how faithful it was to the ship being portrayed."[62]

As a result, the WPA sponsored an innovative series of programs in visual art, writing, theater, and music. Known collectively as Federal Project Number One, or simply Federal One, these programs marked the first time the federal government had ever supported the arts.

Like all the Federal One programs, the Federal Art Project (FAP) was small; only about nine thousand artists and teachers received aid between 1935 and 1943. Its impact on American cultural life, however, was lasting. FAP employees created 2,500 murals and 18,000 pieces of sculpture to decorate public buildings, such as schools, hospitals, and post offices. They produced hundreds of thousands of paintings, prints, and photographs. The agency also organized traveling shows and over 100 community education centers.

Hundreds of gifted artists and photographers, including Jackson Pollock, Louise Nevelson, Diego Rivera, Willem de Kooning, Walker Evans, and Ben Shahn, were able to develop their talents while on the government payroll. In addition, Roosevelt's wish that money spent be returned to the economy was easily fulfilled by the FAP's modest budget. Art experts estimate that within only a few decades, the market value of work produced by FAP artists far exceeded what the project cost.

The FAP had its share of controversy. Many people felt that creating art was not real work—or at least not work that should be supported by government money. Also, murals by Rivera and other left-wing artists were regularly denounced by conservatives as portraying apparently anti-American sentiments. Journalist Robert Bendiner mocks such fears when he reports on an action by authorities at an exclusive private college in Pennsylvania: "It is a fact that Swarthmore College felt obliged to close up a room in which no fewer than six clenched fists were detected in a WPA mural."[63]

Roosevelt's publicly stated opinion of the art project, characteristically, took the middle path:

> Some of it [is] good, some of it not so good. But all of it [is] native, human, eager and alive . . . and painted about things that [the artists] know and look at often and have touched and loved.[64]

Artists employed by the Federal Art Project (FAP) paint a mural in the Federal Art Gallery in New York City in 1939. FAP artists produced hundreds of thousands of works of art.

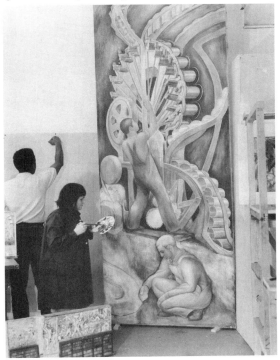

A poster for the WPA's Federal Writers' Project. Although the project produced over one thousand titles, few of the people hired were professional writers.

The Federal Writers' Project (FWP), like the art project, was small but influential. At the same time, the FWP's emphasis on journalism, oral history, and nonfiction allowed it to remain relatively noncontroversial.

Its employees produced millions of copies of about one thousand separate titles. Many of these books, which were distributed free or at low cost, are now considered classics. They include a series of state, city, and regional guides; a 150-volume series entitled *Life in America;* invaluable collections of folklore and storytelling; and an extensive series of interviews with two thousand former slaves.

Only a handful of the ten thousand people hired during the agency's seven years were professional writers; most had been white-collar workers, such as teachers, lawyers, and librarians. Nonetheless, the FWP created an atmosphere that allowed many creative writers to mature into artists of importance.

Among these were Ralph Ellison, Jim Thompson, Margaret Walker, John Cheever, and Nobel laureate Saul Bellow. Richard Wright wrote his influential novel *Native Son* during his spare time while serving as an FWP employee. All in all, historian Page Smith writes, "the writers' project marked a unique event in the nation's history and underlined the New Deal's commitment to the artistic and literary aspects of American life."[65]

Theater and Music

The Federal Theatre Project (FTP) was the most controversial of all the Federal One programs. Under the direction of Hallie Flanagan, formerly the director of an experimental theater at Vassar College, the project emphasized both entertainment and the raising of public awareness of social issues. Its so-called Living Newspapers, for instance, were dramatizations that focused on such topics as slums and public utilities.

The FTP provided work for thousands of unemployed actors, playwrights, directors, and crew members. It produced a wide range of plays staged by semipermanent companies in large cities, and it sent touring groups such as children's actors, puppet shows, and circuses to small towns and rural communities. An estimated thirty million Americans attended free FTP productions during its four years of existence. For many people, it was their first exposure to live theater.

Among the FTP employees who went on to fame in theater or film were Arthur Miller, John Huston, E. G. Marshall, Joseph Cotten, Arlene Francis, and John Houseman. Burt Lancaster got his start as an aerialist in an FTP circus. Orson Welles, still a teenager, directed the agency's most famous production, an innovative staging of *Macbeth* set in Haiti and starring an all-black cast.

The Federal Music Project (FMP), meanwhile, employed about fifteen thousand professional musicians and composers. It commissioned new pieces, organized orchestras—many in cities that had never had them—and sponsored free

Talking About Everything

In this passage reprinted in The New Deal: A Documentary History *(edited by William E. Leuchtenberg), Hallie Flanagan, the director of the WPA's controversial Federal Theatre Project, describes a train trip she made early on with the WPA's dynamic director, Harry Hopkins.*

"It was an exciting trip. Mr. Hopkins talked about everything—about engineering, about the building of airports, about the cities and countryside through which we were passing; but no matter what we started to talk about, it ended up with what was at that time the core and center of his thinking—the relationship of government to the individual. Hadn't our government always acknowledged direct responsibility to the people? Hadn't it given away the national domain in free land to veterans and other settlers? Hadn't it given away vast lands to railroad companies to help them build their systems? Hadn't the government spent fortunes on internal improvements, subsidizing the building of roads and canals, waterways, and harbors? Hadn't the government subsidized infant industries by a protective tariff? Hadn't the government also given away other intangible parts of the public domain, such as franchises to public utilities, the power to issue currency and create credit to banks, patent rights to inventors? In all of these ways, government enlarged industries, put men to work and increased buying power.

The new work program, Mr. Hopkins believed, would accomplish these same ends by giving of the nation's resources in wages to the unemployed, in return for which they would help build and improve America."

concerts and music lessons. This agency is probably the least remembered of all the New Deal arts agencies. It was politically safer than the others and generally did not arouse strong feelings. "Since instrumental music was unlikely to be perceived as carrying leftist messages," historian Robert McElvaine notes, "the FMP remained less controversial." [66]

Still, it did build one especially significant body of work: an enormous field research project, co-led by Charles Seeger of the Music Project and Alan Lomax of the FWP, that collected examples of American popular music and songs in such categories as blues, folk, and bluegrass. These

recordings, preserved in the Library of Congress, have been the basis for many remarkable recordings and are still a priceless source for scholars and lovers of American music.

Criticism of the WPA

Despite its many accomplishments, serious problems still plagued the WPA. Conservatives objected to the leftist tendencies of some of the participants in its arts programs. They were concerned about what they considered wastefulness; the government, these critics complained, was too willing to spend money on useless or inefficient make-work projects called boondoggles. A typical WPA construction project, according to critics, consisted of a group of workmen digging a hole and then filling it up again.

To a degree, charges of waste or inefficiency were justified. But the problem arose from the WPA's emphasis on people over technology, and its goal of providing as many jobs as possible. Of course, it would be cheaper to dig sewer lines with a steam shovel instead of hiring ten laborers with shovels, but the machine operator could find work in the private sector. Government, the WPA supporters contended, was responsible for helping the ten jobless laborers make ends meet.

Liberal critics, meanwhile, also had criticisms of the agency. In particular, they complained that the WPA did not do enough to match workers with jobs, especially blue-collar workers. These critics felt that WPA planners showed a bias against the working class by treating all forms of manual labor the same, assuming that any

A poster advertises a marionette theater sponsored by the Federal Theatre Project (FTP). The FTP employed thousands of actors, playwrights, directors, and crew members.

Roosevelt was an unknown quantity in 1932, and crowds were reserved. In 1936 the response was different, as noted in this passage, reprinted in The FDR Years: On Roosevelt and His Legacy.

"In the early evening the President rode for five miles in an open car through streets so crowded that only a narrow lane was left. . . .

This was King Crowd. They were out to have a large time and they had it. Every kind of band—bagpipers, piano, accordions, jazz, fife-and-drum, bugle corps—lined the narrow lane of humanity through which the presidential party passed. . . . They shrieked from rooftops; they sang and danced; they leaned from tenement windows and left windows to wave and shout. And all the time a rain of torn paper fluttered down, like gray snow in the half-lighted streets."

worker could be matched with any job. As a result, they charged, skilled carpenters and other craftsmen were given jobs washing dishes or picking vegetables.

Still another criticism concerned the agency's requirement that 90 percent of its employees had to be people who were already on relief. This rule was well intentioned, but it had the effect of excluding from the program those who refused, out of pride and stubbornness, to accept relief money. Moreover, critics disliked the rule that allowed only one member of a family to be employed at a time because it discriminated against women and large families.

The most serious criticism of all against the WPA was simply that it did not do enough. The agency was designed to put people to work, but only about 30 percent of the unemployed workforce was on the WPA payroll at any given time. Millions of jobless Americans received no benefit from it.

However, defenders of the WPA say that it served a crucial function in convincing Americans that government could respond to their needs. They also argue that its value in boosting the national spirit was even greater than the tangible things it created. Historian Searle F. Charles summarizes:

The improvement in national morale, the maintenance and improvement of workers' skills, and the preservation of faith in democracy carried a value vastly beyond that of the goods produced, the medical care provided, and the projects completed.[67]

As Roosevelt and his colleagues worked to put his relief programs into action during the second phase of the New Deal, he also pushed forward on other fronts. Several major pieces of legislation were pending, including the Social Security Act; at the same time, his political enemies were rallying to challenge him for the presidency.

6 Social Security, Sick Chickens, and a Second Term of Office

A great forward step in that liberation of humanity which began with the Renaissance.

Labor Secretary Frances Perkins on Social Security

By the 1930s, many European nations had already established social security programs. Retired, unemployed, or disabled Americans, however, were almost completely dependent on private charity or their families.

Roosevelt argued that this situation was immoral; he felt that government-sponsored social security was a basic right of all citizens. "If, as our Constitution tells us, our Federal Government was established, among other things, 'to promote the general welfare,'" he declared, "it is our plain duty to provide for that security upon which welfare depends."[68]

The result of his efforts was perhaps the most crucial piece of legislation to come out of the Second New Deal, the Social Security Act, which was passed in August 1935. This law guaranteed, for the first time in the United States, an income for retired people, financial assistance for dependent children of needy families, unemployment insurance for people who were disabled or out of work, and relief payments for disabled persons that supplemented money received from insufficiently funded state programs.

Social Security

In early 1935 many conservative politicians and business leaders feared that the proposed Social Security Act represented another costly policy handed down by a government that was already interfering too much in private lives. The old-age insurance portion in particular was the subject of long and bitter debate in Congress, but eventually a weakened version of Roosevelt's bill passed.

Critics both conservative and liberal complained that the bill was an imperfect and compromised piece of legislation. For one thing, it excluded some workers who were among those most in need of income protection. FDR needed the support of southern legislators to pass the bill, and these conservatives insisted on exempting farm and domestic workers from coverage.

Also, the plan specified that both employers and employees would pay a percentage of salaries into a fund that would be used for future retirement. Since this system was based on payroll taxes, lower-income workers paid a larger percentage of their wages than did those whose incomes were above a certain maximum taxable level. Critics saw this as unfairly taxing low-income workers.

Despite these flaws, however, the Social Security Act was overall a political and moral victory for the president, who had wanted approval of such a bill for years. Roosevelt declared:

> We can never insure one hundred percent of the population against one hundred percent of the hazards and vicissitudes [difficult changes] of life, but we have tried to frame a law which will give some measure of protection to the average citizen and his family against the loss of a job and against poverty-ridden old age.[69]

Most historians consider the Social Security Act to be one of the New Deal's crowning achievements, setting a standard in the use of governmental power to help the average man and woman. Social Security, along with the WPA, served another purpose as well: restoring FDR's popularity with voters. Robert McElvaine points out that, despite its flaws, the bill was popular with a majority of Americans:

> A system that excluded the neediest [and] took money from workers . . . was something less than a model for progressive legislation. Yet the Social Security Act helped, in combination with other parts of the Second New Deal, to win back for Roosevelt the allegiance of the forgotten man.[70]

From Blue Eagles to Sick Chickens

Offsetting the successes of the WPA and Social Security, Roosevelt encountered during

An editorial cartoon pokes fun at the new Social Security Act. The act was extremely popular with voters, despite criticism by opponents.

this period a serious setback: the collapse of the National Recovery Administration.

The NRA had never worked well. Almost no one in business, labor, politics, or the voting public was happy with its cumbersome codes or with a bureaucracy that was powerless to enforce those codes. Critics had long suggested new meanings for the agency's initials: "National Run Around," "No Recovery Allowed," "Nuts Running America." African-American leaders, angry at what they saw as discrimination within the NRA, called it "Negroes Ruined Again."

At its start in 1933, the agency had been authorized for a two-year period. As the end of this time neared, a number of suggestions were made about reshaping the NRA.

Roosevelt's New Deal policies were extremely controversial during his term, and their long-term effects are often debated today.

Then the Supreme Court announced a decision that sealed the agency's fate: the National Industrial Recovery Act (NIRA), the law that had led to the creation of the NRA, was declared unconstitutional, and, therefore, the agency itself could no longer exist.

The case that led to this decision was *Schechter Poultry Corp. v. United States.* The Schechter company had been charged with violating several NRA codes, including one governing the sale of diseased poultry. The dispute, which elicited tremendous publicity, was generally referred to in the papers as "the sick chicken" case.

A Serious Blow

The Court ruled that Congress, by giving code-writing authority to the NRA, had improperly delegated its legislative powers. The government's lawyers had attempted to justify the application of NRA codes to the Schechter chicken business by citing the commerce clause of the Constitution, which gives Congress the power to regulate interstate trade, that is, trade among the different states. The Court, in effect, said that the commerce clause was irrelevant here because the parts of the NRA code that Schechter was accused of violating related to the company's business in New York State only, that is, its intrastate activities.

The decision was a blow to Roosevelt and others who had hoped to use the commerce clause as a means of introducing additional federal regulations of trade. The emotions of the New Dealers were summed up in a headline from the London *Daily Express*: AMERICA STUNNED: ROOSEVELT'S TWO YEARS' WORK KILLED IN TWENTY MINUTES.[71]

The Supreme Court and the Sick Chickens

This passage is from the majority opinion of the Supreme Court concerning Schechter Poultry Corp. v. United States, *the 1935 "sick chicken" case that declared the National Industrial Recovery Act unconstitutional and dealt a major blow to the New Deal. Chief Justice Charles Evans Hughes wrote the opinion.*

"Schechter Poultry Corporation and Schechter Live Poultry Market are corporations conducting wholesale poultry slaughterhouse markets in Brooklyn, New York City. . . . [They] do not sell poultry in interstate commerce. . . .

We are told [by the government] that the provision of the statute authorizing the adoption of codes must be viewed in the light of the grave national crisis with which Congress was confronted. . . . Extraordinary conditions may call for extraordinary remedies. But the argument necessarily stops short of an attempt to justify action which lies outside the sphere of constitutional authority. Extraordinary conditions do not create or enlarge constitutional power. . . . The Congress is not permitted to abdicate or to transfer to others the essential legislative functions with which it is . . . vested. . . . [The need for flexibility in coping with complex situations the Congress cannot deal with directly] cannot be allowed to obscure the limitations of the authority to delegate. . . . Such a delegation [as represented by the NRA] is unknown to our law and is utterly inconsistent with the constitutional prerogatives and duties of Congress. . . . We think that the code-making authority thus conferred is an unconstitutional delegation of legislative power. . . .

On both the grounds [of] the attempted delegation of legislative power, and the attempted regulation of intrastate transactions which affect interstate commerce only indirectly, we hold the code provisions here in questions to be invalid."

According to an American Federation of Labor study, a million workers were immediately affected by the end of the codes. Retailers and wholesalers in all aspects of business ignored NRA price controls and resumed their highly competitive price wars. Businesses everywhere lengthened work hours and cut wages. Within two weeks of the Court's decision, for example, a majority of grocery clerks were back to working 65 to 72 hours per week, rather than the NRA-imposed limit of 48 hours.

Opponents of the New Deal were delighted. The conservative *New York Herald-*

Tribune thundered, "Tyranny is overthrown." The *Christian Science Monitor,* however, mourned the loss of the NRA's positive qualities, noting that it "did accomplish much to put a bottom under sweat-shop wages, to abolish child labor, and bring a semblance of fair competition into demoralized trade." [72]

Publicly, Roosevelt was furious, condemning what he called the Court's old-fashioned "horse-and-buggy" attitude toward the distinction between intrastate and interstate commerce. Some historians, however, argue that the sick chicken case actually helped the president politically. It allowed FDR to abandon a failing agency and to blame its failure on the "nine old men" of the Supreme Court. "It is difficult to avoid the suspicion that Roosevelt was inwardly relieved when the Court executed the Blue Eagle," Robert McElvaine writes. McElvaine also notes a comment FDR made privately to Labor Secretary Frances Perkins: "You know the whole thing is a mess. It has been an awful headache. . . . I think perhaps [the] NRA has done all it can do." [73]

Running for a Second Term

Roosevelt was exhausted by the end of the difficult congressional session that summer and suffered from severe headaches and irritability, though he avoided showing any distress in public. FDR had reason

FDR and his cabinet in 1936, when FDR was running for a second term. The presidential election brought out many of Roosevelt's critics.

Listening, Weighing, and Synthesizing

Frank Freidel, in Franklin D. Roosevelt: A Rendezvous with Destiny, *gives this illustration of how Roosevelt worked with his advisers to find compromise solutions to legislative problems.*

"Moley presided over a group of experts . . . and assigned each a specific problem or problems. . . . Roosevelt also turned for advice to numerous others outside of this group, sometimes setting them to work on parallel or at times even contrary projects. Thus individuals or teams planned legislation . . . under mandates [instructions] from Roosevelt. Only he in the final analysis knew in total what the overall program was and who was working upon it. . . .

In the end he could weigh the competing plans, and move from his initial enthusiasm for what was fresh or even bizarre to a more conservative choice of what might be acceptable to Congress. Or, as often was the case . . . he would synthesize them all into a single bulging parcel."

to be tired. In addition to dealing with Social Security, the WPA, and sick chickens, he was also gearing up for the 1936 presidential election, and the race looked to be a tough one.

In 1932 Roosevelt had been generally liberal; during the Second New Deal, he had moved more to the middle of the road. Now, as the presidential race took shape, radical figures from both the far left and the far right emerged as major rivals. James M. Burns, Alan Brinkley, and other historians have referred to these threats as "thunder on the left" and "thunder on the right," reflecting the opinions of those who felt Roosevelt had not done enough and those who thought he had done far too much.

Even longtime Democrats, disenchanted with the president's performance, were pulling away from him. Public opin-ion samples, which were just coming into general use in 1935, suggested that Republicans had reason to be optimistic about their chances. Meanwhile, a maverick third party was gaining strength.

Many political observers mistrusted Roosevelt and charged that his actions were motivated only by the need to regain votes. Even those sympathetic to the New Deal were sometimes disillusioned. The influential Kiplinger political newsletter recorded some of the words and phrases its reporters claimed were being used by disgruntled Democratic leaders in Washington, including: "delusions of power, dictatorial, intoxicated by authority, itch to try new things, surrounded by picked yes-men, out of touch with popular sentiment."[74]

Among the more prominent dissenting voices were those of Father Charles Coughlin and Dr. Francis Townsend. Coughlin

In 1936 Huey P. Long ran for president on a platform that was socialist in nature and included the idea of redistributing wealth, land, and property.

was a Roman Catholic priest, known as the Radio Preacher, whose poisonously anti-Roosevelt broadcasts attracted huge audiences—for a time, audiences even larger than those of FDR's fireside chats. Town-send was a retired physician from California who developed a plan to bring prosperity to America by creating government pensions for the elderly.

Neither was able to muster a serious campaign against the president, however. Instead, a more serious threat to Roosevelt's leadership came from his own party.

The Kingfish

Huey P. Long, a former governor of Louisiana, liked to call himself "the Kingfish." Now a U.S. senator, Long cultivated a clownish country style; he was a large, loud, and amiable man with a weakness for flashy suits and colorful ties. But the Kingfish was also a shrewd lawyer and an able politician who maintained tight control over his state despite serious charges of corruption.

Instead of the New Deal, Long advocated a program he called the Share Our Wealth plan. In addition to less radical platform items such as college scholarships, increased public works spending, and benefits for labor, Long proposed a limit on individual wealth. Personal income beyond a set amount would be redistributed among all citizens, and needy families would each be guaranteed a home, a car, and a radio. His slogan was "Every Man a King."

Long even suggested redistributing land and other property, though how this massive transfer would be handled was never clear. "No, sir, money is not all of it by a jugful," he would tell reporters.

> We are going to redistribute in kind so the poor devil who needs a house can get one from some rich bird who has too many houses; so the man who needs a bedstead can get one from the man who has more than he will ever need.[75]

Long's catchy ideas and informal style appealed powerfully to those who believed that government intervention was really a giant conspiracy to get money from ordinary folks. Roosevelt was never fooled by Long's clownish air and took him seriously as a rival for the Democratic nomination. The rivalry came to an abrupt end, however, when Long was assassinated in September 1935 by a political enemy from Louisiana.

A Landslide Second Election

Another contender for FDR's position, of course, was the Republican Party's nominee for president: Alf Landon, the governor of Kansas. Landon, who had entered politics as a member of Theodore Roosevelt's Bull Moose Party, was not a rabble-rouser or a radical; he was a capable and moderate administrator who had the approval of the majority of his party.

In some ways, the prospects seemed good for Landon. A majority of the nation's newspapers were endorsing him. Also, wealthy conservatives contributed huge sums for Landon's campaign while the Democrats were finding it difficult to raise funds.

Landon and the other challengers caused Roosevelt to worry privately that he might not prevail. Publicly, however, FDR maintained his usual air of unflappable confidence and tenacity. During his final speech of the campaign, speaking to a madly cheering crowd at New York's Madison Square Garden, he thundered:

> I should like to have it said of my first Administration that in it the forces of selfishness and of lust for power met their match. I should like to have it said—[thunderous applause]—Wait a moment! I should like to have it said of my second Administration that in it these forces met their master![76]

A sensible and moderate governor from Kansas, Alf Landon ran against FDR in the 1936 presidential election.

"Ill-Housed, Ill-Clad, Ill-Nourished"

In his second inaugural address in 1937, a portion of which is reprinted in Franklin D. Roosevelt: A Rendezvous with Destiny *by Frank Freidel, Roosevelt had spoken of America's basic strength, acknowledging that much remained to be done.*

"I see a great nation, upon a great continent, blessed with a great wealth of natural resources. . . . I see a United States which can demonstrate that, under democratic methods of government, national wealth can be translated into a spreading volume of human comforts hitherto unknown, and the lowest standard of living can be raised far above the level of mere subsistence.

But here is the challenge to our democracy: In this nation I see tens of millions of its citizens—a substantial part of its whole population—who at this very moment are denied the greater part of what the very lowest standards of today call the necessities of life. . . .

I see one-third of a nation ill-housed, ill-clad, ill-nourished."

As it turned out, Roosevelt's worries about reelection were in vain. Editorial writers and political radicals may have been against him, but the vast majority of voters were not. In fact, FDR entitled the 1936 volume of his official papers *The People Approve.*

That November he was swept back into office by another overwhelming landslide. Every state in the union except for Maine and Vermont voted for the incumbent; Alf Landon did not even carry his home state of Kansas.

The election was a tremendous boost for Roosevelt and his policies. Despite incomplete recovery from the depression, it was clear that a majority of Americans still had faith in him. The next period consolidated that trust, as FDR continued to steer the country toward recovery and began the painful process of entering a conflict that would become a global war.

7 The War Arrives, the New Deal Ends

The New Deal had no climax; like the old soldier (or sailor) Franklin Roosevelt had always wanted to be, it simply faded away.
Robert McElvaine

Despite Roosevelt's victory and a large congressional gain for Democrats in the same election, the president's second term of office was not smooth. It was during this period, in fact, that the New Deal essentially ended.

Roosevelt encountered a long string of frustrating failures during this slow waning of the era. Some pieces of legislation, including bills to reorganize the executive (presidential) branch of government and to strengthen labor regulations, were relatively successful. Others, in particular the so-called court-packing scheme, were outright disasters.

The End in Sight

Overall, the president, and the nation, became increasingly preoccupied with the threat of war. Even the serious problems of the depression seemed insignificant compared with this alarming possibility. And it was the massive buildup of national industrial capacity preceding America's entry into World War II that was the turning point that finally ended the economic hard times and closed the New Deal.

Still Self-Confident

In his second inaugural address in January 1937, Roosevelt spoke of the New Deal's many accomplishments, but he also acknowledged that much remained undone: "I see one-third of a nation ill-housed, ill-clad, ill-nourished."[77]

Still, the president was overall even more confident than usual. He felt that his huge victory had given him a mandate from America—that is, approval for his actions. Robert McElvaine comments, "Understandably, [the landslide] convinced the President that his popularity was immense and that he could do no wrong. He believed the public would always be on his side."[78]

However, Roosevelt overestimated his strengths and underestimated the power of his opponents. As he moved to consolidate his authority and push through new legislation, he acted in ways that to some observers, both then and now, appear reckless or ill-advised.

To a degree, this was probably because FDR assumed his second term would be

The Supreme Court poses for a somber photograph in 1937. During his presidency, Roosevelt sought ways to change the Court, whose appointees were unsympathetic to the New Deal policies.

his last. By custom, no other president had ever run for a third term, although the Twenty-second Amendment, ruling out this option, was not ratified until 1951. Since he was not worrying about the 1940 election, Roosevelt did not have to cultivate the support of Congress as carefully as before. Also, many longtime advisers, including most of the original Brain Trust, had left government for various reasons. The changing array of people who filled the gap did not have the powerful influence of the original group.

Roosevelt thus felt freer to choose his own path than he had during his first term. "He looked upon his presumably last term," Frank Freidel writes, "less as mean-

ing a decline in power over Congress than as endowing him with independence, both from Congress and from previous advisers in the White House."[79]

The Court-Packing Plan

For most of its existence, the Supreme Court had exercised restraint in its rulings on federal laws. Since the earliest days of the country, the Court had blocked congressional bills only a handful of times.

In the decade before the New Deal, however, the Court had grown more active. By the time the New Deal arrived, the

Supreme Court justices were not only aware of their tremendous power over American law; they were not afraid to use it. As Chief Justice Charles Evans Hughes remarked, "We are under a Constitution, but the Constitution is what the judges say it is."[80]

Throughout Roosevelt's terms, conservative justices appointed by earlier, Republican presidents formed a majority. These judges were generally unsympathetic to New Deal programs and were increasingly a serious obstacle to FDR. The Court had killed the NRA, and it was indicating it might invalidate other major programs, including the TVA and Social Security.

Supreme Court justices are appointed for life and rarely resign. During his first term, Roosevelt had not had an opportunity to appoint new justices who might have helped his cause, and it did not appear that he would have a chance during his second

term. He therefore began thinking about ways to alter the character of the Court.

In early 1937 FDR unveiled a proposal to enlarge the Court from nine to fifteen judges, adding one whenever any of the nine then sitting on the bench reached the age of seventy without retiring. A similar setup would create younger appointees elsewhere in the federal court system as well.

Roosevelt justified his plan by saying the courts needed a younger, fresher perspective. He asserted that his system would ease the workload of aging justices and streamline operations. In his message to Congress, FDR argued that the aging justices and their colleagues lower on the judicial benches had remained

far beyond their years or physical capacity. . . . A constant and systematic

FDR lunches in his car while touring the nation. In spite of his popularity with the public, FDR's efforts to change the number of Supreme Court justices made him extremely unpopular with both Republicans and Democrats.

addition of younger blood will vitalize the courts and better equip them to recognize and apply the essential concepts of justice in the light of the needs and facts of an ever-changing world.[81]

A Rare Failure

FDR's plan was perfectly legal. The Constitution does not specify how many members the Supreme Court must have, and Congress had changed the number several times in the previous century.

Nonetheless, the proposal encountered instant and fiery opposition from conservatives, who denounced it as "court-packing" that would load the Court in Roosevelt's favor. "Of course I shall oppose it," one of the Republicans in Congress, Senator Carter Glass, told reporters, "but I don't imagine for a minute that it'll do any good. Why, if the President asked Congress to commit suicide tomorrow they'd do it."[82]

Glass's assumption that Democrats in Congress would support Roosevelt was wrong. For one thing, FDR's allies in Congress were insulted that he had announced his plan without consulting them first. They were angry for other reasons as well. They worried that the plan would change the balance of power between the judicial and executive branches of government. And, at a time when fascist leaders in Europe were gaining frightening power, many were distressed by what they saw as Roosevelt's attempt to gain control of the country's highest court.

Roosevelt's standing in the public eye also suffered. Few people believed him

An editorial cartoon depicts Democrats (whose mascot is the donkey) abandoning Roosevelt after he asks for an additional six justices to compose the Supreme Court.

when he said that he was simply trying to streamline the court system. For one thing, many pointed out, advanced age did not necessarily mean a conservative outlook. Louis Brandeis, who at over eighty was the oldest justice, was a dedicated liberal and a consistent New Deal supporter.

Roosevelt's reputation for integrity was a crucial element in his phenomenal popularity. Now, it seemed to many voters, the president was quite openly trying to fool them. Roosevelt eventually admitted that the real reason for the plan was his belief that the Court was blocking efforts to improve the welfare of Americans, but outrage over the issue continued to mount.

In the end, the issue died away after a series of incidents. One conservative justice retired and a key Senate leader who had been helping FDR died. Then the Court—perhaps reacting to Roosevelt's threat—upheld several crucial pieces of New Deal legislation. Over the next four years, Roosevelt was able to appoint seven new justices, including the distinguished jurists Felix Frankfurter, William O. Douglas, and Hugo Black.

A High Cost

Roosevelt got what he wanted, a more liberal Court, but he paid a high price. He wasted valuable time and energy. He alienated a largely Democratic Congress that should have been supportive. He handed strong ammunition to his political enemies. And, finally, he damaged his reputation as a trustworthy and nearly invincible leader. The court-packing plan is generally regarded as a misstep that caused permanent damage to Roosevelt's

other programs. Robert McElvaine comments, "This, it may safely be said, was not Franklin Roosevelt's finest hour. . . . The New Deal, what was left of it, would never be the same."[83]

Executive Reorganization

As Roosevelt fought the Court battle, he waged a more successful war to reorganize the executive branch of government, the branch directly under the president.

Part of this proposal called for six executive assistants to lighten the president's personal workload. Roosevelt also wanted to streamline the system so that departments could be grouped together more logically. He asked for several new cabinet-level agencies, including one devoted to welfare. Finally, he proposed that an advisory council, the National Resources Board, be made into a more powerful agency, the National Resources Planning Board, with the authority to coordinate large issues of national planning.

Such reordering was, Roosevelt argued, desperately needed. The hodgepodge of agencies and legislation created during the New Deal was overloading the existing civil service structure. New laws and organizations often conflicted with each other.

This time, the public reacted more favorably to the president's reorganization plans. In restructuring the executive branch, FDR was seen as motivated by a genuine desire for greater good, rather than personal gain or political advantage. Frank Freidel comments, "Roosevelt seemed bent upon achieving what from a standpoint of responsible public administration would be an ideal structure. . .

Workers strike at an auto body plant in 1937. Labor unions gained in number and power during the 1930s.

rather than upon placating [soothing] conflicting political pressure groups."[84]

Another Compromise

However, the bill was not well received by Congress or by bureaucrats within the government. Seasoned professionals like Harold Ickes and Frances Perkins felt the proposed changes threatened their own departments. Legislators were also reluctant to weaken their own power by shifting programs to the executive branch. Missouri congressman Dewey Short, concerned that the new executive assistants would have too much power, warned that assurances to the contrary were worth nothing "when they come from men who care no more for their word than a tomcat cares for a marriage license in a back alley on a dark night."[85]

The bill was argued at length in Congress, and when it finally passed in 1939,

the measure was seriously watered down. It eliminated many of Roosevelt's original plans, including the creation of a cabinet-level welfare leader. However, it did give the president power to create a National Resources Planning Board and an Office of Emergency Management; it also moved the Bureau of the Budget directly under the president's control and made other changes that streamlined operations.

Probably the bill's biggest boost to the president was its stipulation regarding executive assistants. This let Roosevelt replace his improvised White House administration with six new executive assistants. Each of these assistants had a clearly defined role, and the overall operation was much more efficient.

Roosevelt insisted that his new assistants have "a passion for anonymity." In other words, they should be content to help the president with his work while shunning the limelight. Roosevelt took this requirement seriously. When a newspaper reported that one assistant had been seen at a cocktail party, Roosevelt told the assistant, "If I read this too often, you will need another job."[86]

The reorganization law set the basic model for the existing executive office structure. However, its weakened final form was an indication of Roosevelt's fluctuating power to reshape government.

Labor

During the 1930s, organized labor grew dramatically. The unions began to have a powerful effect on elected politicians; since many new union members were recent immigrants, African Americans, and others who had seen discrimination on the job and in their private lives, the shift in power was toward the political left. Organized labor's voting power significantly altered the nation's political outlook; in the opinion of historian Nelson Lichtenstein,

its rise "was the most important social phenomenon of the Roosevelt era."[87]

Trade unions often made their feelings known in ways other than voting. In the mid-1930s, workers shook the country with a series of crippling strikes. In Milwaukee, streetcar workers walked off the job and disabled dozens of streetcars. In Philadelphia, cabdrivers burned a hundred taxis, and in New York, cabbies staged a riot that included driving most of the city's fifteen thousand taxis off the streets.

Farmworkers, cooks, autoworkers, and dozens of other professions followed suit by staging walkouts in protest of issues such as poor pay and dangerous working conditions. These strikes often turned violent as angry workers, sometimes aided by communist or socialist activists, confronted police, National Guard troops, and local militia.

Many business owners also hired private armies to enforce order in the workplace, using violence if necessary to stop disturbances quickly. The probusiness

A strike turns violent as strikers and scabs clash on the picket line.

editor of a textile journal, anticipating strikes in his industry, took a harsh view: "A few hundred funerals will have a quieting influence."[88]

The tense situation peaked in the spring of 1937 with two bloody encounters. At Ford's River Rouge plant in Dearborn, Michigan, hired enforcers severely beat union organizers as newspaper photographers took pictures and police stood by. At the Republic Steel Company in Chicago, police used pistols and clubs on a crowd of strikers and sympathizers; ten men died, none of them policemen, and a hundred more were wounded.

Roosevelt had so far publicly commented little on the issue of strikes, but these incidents finally provoked him to make a statement. In a diplomatic comment that cast blame evenly and reflected the nation's weariness with the violence, he told reporters that Americans as a whole were saying to the warring factions, "'A plague on both your houses.'"[89]

Labor and Business, Wages and Hours

The last major pieces of New Deal legislation focused on the adversarial relationship between business and labor.

The National Labor Relations Act (popularly known as the Wagner Act after Robert Wagner, the senator from New York

Women in a garment factory are hard at work. During the 1930s, labor unions won many improvements for workers, including guidelines for minimum wages and maximum hours.

who sponsored it) sought to change the workplace without resorting to violence. It created the National Labor Relations Board (NLRB), which works to solve problems between business groups and labor through such means as contract negotiation.

Overall, the board was successful at stemming violent clashes. Its generally pro-labor attitude alienated many business leaders, although FDR more than made up for their lack of support by gaining powerful allies in organized labor.

A related bill, the Fair Labor Standards Act of 1938, finally succeeded in doing what the NRA could not: establishing federal guidelines for minimum wages and maximum hours. Conservatives had long opposed such measures, feeling that the right to make such decisions belonged to the states by virtue of the Tenth Amendment. Roosevelt, however, had long championed a national law to end low pay and long hours.

The Wages and Hours Act, as the bill was known, set the minimum wage at twenty-five cents an hour, increasing to forty cents over the next seven years. It called for extra pay for overtime work and reduced the average workweek from forty-four hours to forty. It also prohibited the employment of children under sixteen in most occupations, with eighteen the limit for hazardous jobs.

In order to secure the bill's passage, New Dealers had to accept serious compromises. For example, legislators concerned about preserving low-wage pools in their home territories succeeded in excluding many occupations from the bill; these included retail and service employees, local transportation personnel, people in the fishing and agricultural industries, seasonal workers, domestic workers, and farm laborers. So many jobs were left out that one conservative congressman sarcastically suggested an amendment stating, "Within 90 days after appointment of the Administrator [Secretary of Labor Frances Perkins], she shall report to Congress whether anyone is subject to this bill."[90]

Though it was weak, the Wages and Hours law immediately helped some twelve million workers who had previously made less than the new minimum wage, who worked extremely long hours, or both. It also furthered one of the New Deal's goals: the active role of government in regulating the workplace. The battle to establish this was long and hard, and the president did not sign a final bill into law until June 1938.

The Waning of the WPA

As the Wages and Hours bill and other measures worked their way through Congress, other aspects of the New Deal were winding down. By early 1937 it appeared to many that the need for relief was no longer urgent. Production, stock prices, and profits were on the rise. It seemed to many that the economic emergency had finally passed.

The federal budget had rapidly increased during the New Deal years. Many people, FDR included, now felt that the economy was stable enough to justify trimming the budget. By the summer of 1937, the WPA budget was half its previous size and the PWA was virtually extinct. Many works projects employees were put on direct relief. This significantly cut the budget, since direct relief is cheaper than

Penniless and stranded, a young mother from Oklahoma sits in a California migrant camp in this 1937 photograph. The late 1930s saw a return to economic troubles.

works projects. On the other hand, the move reduced the overall standard of living, and unemployment remained high.

Despite the reductions, conservatives continued to object to the WPA. In particular, the Federal Theatre Project came under attack by the House Un-American Activities Committee, which was conducting a larger investigation into unpatriotic activities, and by other right-wing observers. The chairman of the committee, a staunchly anti-Roosevelt congressman named Martin Dies, called the Federal One projects "a hotbed for Communists."[91] Meanwhile, historian Page Smith notes,

> the Hearst newspapers . . . denounced [WPA] plays as "the most outrageous misuse of taxpayers' money that the Roosevelt administration had been guilty of," while the [New York] *Herald Tribune* declared the productions were "run by reds [Communists]," a charge which, if irrelevant to the quality of the

productions, had at least a grain of truth in it.[92]

All of the works projects programs gradually tapered off. In 1939 the FTP became the first of the arts projects to be dismantled. That summer Roosevelt reorganized the remaining Works Progress Administration and renamed it the Work Projects Administration to emphasize concrete achievements rather than welfare. In its reduced form, the WPA limped along until it was finally dismantled in 1943. The agency, Roosevelt declared, had served America well and had earned its "honorable discharge."[93]

Hard Times Again

Just as the country's financial situation was improving in mid-1937, with the economy on the rise and the budget being trimmed, both the overall statistics and the lives of individual citizens took a turn for the worse.

Figures for manufacturing, sales, and employment suddenly dropped. The hardships continued into the winter; the bad old days were returning. In Chicago, for instance, the number of families on relief tripled in five months. By March 1938 four million new names were on already bulging national unemployment lists. Historian W. Elliot Brownlee writes, "The nation seemed close to returning to 1933 conditions."[94]

Many observers feel that the economic downturn was due to FDR's cutbacks in spending. "There are numbers of explanations for this recession," William E. Leuchtenberg writes, "but the biggest one is that Roosevelt, for all of his willingness to spend in an emergency, continued to believe in balancing the budget."[95]

In part, this belief was personal. Reporter Anne O'Hare McCormick noted that part of Roosevelt's character was "the Dutch householder who carefully totes up his accounts every month." But FDR also felt that it was an essential part of good government. He expressed this view in a cabinet meeting: "I have said fifty times that the budget will [continue to] be balanced. . . . If you want me to say it again, I will say it either once or fifty times more."[96]

FDR disliked the alternative to a balanced budget, which is deficit spending. "Deficit spending" is the term for government expenditures that cannot be paid for with available funds. It is planned indebtedness. Governments use deficit spending

Retreat or Advance?

In his final address of the 1940 presidential campaign, reprinted in William E. Leuchtenberg's Franklin Delano Roosevelt and the New Deal, *FDR spoke movingly of the future.*

"This generation of Americans is living in a tremendous moment of history. The surge of events abroad has made some few doubters among us ask: Is this the end of a story that has been told? Is the book of democracy now to be closed and placed away upon the dusty shelves of time?

My answer is this: All we have known of the glories of democracy—its freedom, its efficiency as a mode of living, its ability to meet the aspirations of the common man—all these are merely an introduction to the greater story of a more glorious future.

We Americans of today—all of us—we are characters in the living book of democracy. But we are also its author. It falls upon us now to say whether the chapters that are to come will tell a story of retreat or a story of continued advance."

as a method of maintaining a steady economy without significantly raising taxes.

Early in 1938 Roosevelt finally decided to abandon a balanced budget. He asked Congress to approve a massive program to "prime the pump" of the economy. This phrase, borrowed from the British economist John Maynard Keynes, is often replaced in current economic discussions by the phrase "jump-start." Substantial increases were made in money for the WPA, Civilian Conservation Corps, public works, and other projects. For the first time, FDR's budget expenditures were greater than the national income.

The strategy worked: the economy stabilized, prices rose, and by summer recovery was again under way. Roosevelt had hoped to keep the deficit temporary. Instead, the nation's deficit spending has continued to grow.

War on Another Front

World War II broke out in Europe in September 1939, and a majority of Americans looked to their president to handle the crisis as he had the depression: sometimes

FDR on the campaign trail in 1940. Just a year after World War II broke out, Americans reelected Roosevelt to the presidency, placing their trust in him during this time of crisis.

"A New Deal War"

Conservatives argue that Roosevelt used wartime measures to foster government intervention in business affairs and private lives, as John Willson states in "How World War II Saved the New Deal."

"FDR ran a New Deal war. . . .

By 1943, government boards and agencies could (and did) tell Americans how much they could drive, what they could manufacture and how much, whether they could change jobs, raise rents, eat beef, or stay on the streets at night. Government built housing and tore it down, reorganized the entire automobile industry, created aluminum companies, and withheld new tires from trucks carrying . . . items like liquor, cigarettes, and Orange Crush."

---

cautiously, sometimes recklessly, but always with hope and confidence. In 1940 the Democrats nominated Franklin Roosevelt again, and he defeated Republican Wendell Willkie to become the first person to be elected to a third term as president of the United States.

Nazi and fascist forces, led by Adolf Hitler and Benito Mussolini, were threatening the whole of Europe. America was still neutral, but it was helping England, France, and the other Allies, as the anti-Nazi forces were called, through the so-called lend-lease program. With this plan, the United States manufactured and "lent" to the Allies (on a deferred payment scheme) huge amounts of guns, ammunition, ships, aircraft, and other war material. At the same time, as the chances grew that America would have to enter the war, Roosevelt began planning his nation's own military buildup.

Many of Roosevelt's critics condemned the military buildup, arguing that the pres-ident was using the war in Europe as an excuse to create an artificial emergency that would mask a power grab. One Republican leader, Ohio senator Robert A. Taft, went so far as to warn that "additional powers sought by the President in case of war . . . would create a socialist dictatorship which it would be impossible to dissolve once the war is over."[97]

Nonetheless, Roosevelt was able to rally most of the nation behind his efforts. Ironically, it was his massive spending on military needs, rather than social goals, that finally achieved the national prosperity FDR had so long sought.

Unprecedented amounts of deficit spending were required to bring the defense industry up to speed, and this gave the economy the boost it needed. America's entry into the war after the Japanese attack on Pearl Harbor, late in 1941, kicked the war industry into high gear. Industrial production soared 30 percent above its 1929 level. Jobs were plentiful as

The war effort put people back to work, including women and minorities.

the defense industry hired in massive numbers. America was back at work, rallied around a common cause, and, for all intents and purposes, the Great Depression was over.

From "Dr. New Deal" to "Dr. Win-the-War"

The war effort eliminated the need for virtually all the New Deal programs, and they gradually tapered off. By Christmastime 1943 the country was in the grim depths of

battle, but an Allied victory looked likely. Roosevelt chose this time to announce the end of the New Deal as it was known. In a press conference, he told reporters that he planned to exchange "Dr. New Deal" with "Dr. Win-the-War."

He was not, however, willing to let the New Deal go entirely. Instead, he hoped someday to extend and deepen its influence. In his annual message early in 1944, FDR stated that it was time for Americans to plan on a lasting peace. This future would include a living standard so high, he said, that it would not leave even "some fraction of our people—whether it be one-third or one-fifth or one-tenth . . . ill-fed, ill-clothed, ill-housed, and insecure." He went on to outline what he called a Second Bill of Rights. These new rights, he stated, included the right to earn an adequate living, to have a decent home, adequate medical care, a good education, and protection from economic uncertainty. They would establish, he said, "a new basis of security and prosperity . . . for all—regardless of station, race, or creed."[98]

The president had been gravely ill for some months and was not well enough to deliver this message to Congress in person. Despite his failing health, however, Roosevelt won a fourth term of office in 1944 against Republican Thomas E. Dewey.

In April 1945 Roosevelt died at his second home in Warm Springs, Georgia. He did not live to see the end of the war. The task of seeing America through the conflict's end fell to FDR's successor, Harry S Truman. The goals of "Dr. New Deal," meanwhile, became the concerns of future presidents, notably John F. Kennedy and Lyndon B. Johnson, who were deeply concerned with social reforms, as well as to the many others who have continued to preserve and promote the aims of the New Deal.

Assessing the New Deal

> *One day the world, and history, will know what it owes to your President.*
>
> Winston Churchill to newsman Edward R. Murrow on the death of FDR

The New Deal had a permanent and deeply felt effect on the American political landscape. This is perhaps especially significant in light of its many obstacles and despite Roosevelt's failure to meet some of his original goals.

The New Deal did not restore a strong economy to the country, though it did lift America out of the worst of its hard times. Nor did it end the Great Depression, which continued to burden the country until the mobilization for World War II ushered in production and jobs on a massive scale.

The New Deal did not completely relieve hunger and unemployment; as it wound down, millions of Americans were still suffering. Nor did it secure a comfortable lifestyle for all Americans, creating a minimum standard of living for the poor.

Nonetheless, the achievements of the New Deal were numerous and dramatic. According to historian Alan Brinkley, the New Deal had many failures but "enough successes to establish it as the most important episode of the twentieth century in the creation of the modern American state."[99]

The New Deal Today

Many of the policies and ideas that took shape during the 1930s survive today. Indeed, it is hard to find an aspect of American life that is not somehow affected by New Deal philosophy or is not directly traceable to New Deal policies.

The ways in which government regulates the business and daily life of America are prime examples. Anyone with a job, whether a first-timer or a longtime employee, is guaranteed certain wages, working conditions, and rights in the workplace, all as a result of New Deal legislation. Disabled, needy, and out-of-work people receive government money to see them through hard times, thanks to the Social Security Act. Men and women who have served in the armed forces are eligible for college scholarships through the GI Bill, a descendant of New Deal policy.

New Deal reforms also protect consumers from unsound or unethical practices in financial areas such as banking and the stock market, and from fraudulent practices such as false advertising. Legislation stemming from the New Deal sets minimum safety codes for newly constructed houses as well as for schools, hospitals, and other buildings. Federal agencies begun in

A Transformation

In this passage from FDR: A Centenary Remembrance, *writer Joseph Alsop reflects on the enormous change in American society that FDR helped bring about.*

"I do not believe that the real essence of Roosevelt's achievement on the home front is to be found in the list of new federal agencies he founded, or in the new balance of power between the business community and the government which he sought and obtained, or even in the inauguration of the American version of the welfare state, for which he is responsible. Instead, the essence of his achievement, at least that part of his achievement which gave the whole true grandeur, derived in differing degrees and in hardly perceptible ways from the combined impact of all his domestic reforms. . . .

It is not easy to grasp how enormous the contrast is between the United States of today and the United States whose leadership Roosevelt assumed in a time of deep trouble after the 1932 election. The truth is that the America Roosevelt was born into in 1882 . . . and even the America of 1932, was an entirely White Anglo-Saxon Protestant nation by any practical test. . . .

It is hard to credit, and few remember, that these conditions and restrictions [existed so fully]. . . . It is not easy, either, to pinpoint precisely how everything was transformed during Franklin Roosevelt's terms in office. Yet there can be no doubt that he wrought the transformation by direct and indirect means; and there can be no doubt, either, that he was furiously blamed for it. This was the real reason rich Americans 'went to hiss Roosevelt' at newsreel theaters, because they truly hated him. This is why he was called 'a traitor to his class.'"

Eleanor and Franklin Roosevelt, accompanied by their son James, arrive at the White House for FDR's 1933 inauguration.

The Legacy of the Arts Projects

The Federal One arts projects, and the WPA of which it was a part, left a lasting legacy on the country. In The Great Depression *Robert McElvaine amplifies:*

"Their service to the nation was invaluable, but it has been widely recognized only since the 1960s. The arts projects collected a huge amount of raw material that has proved to be of enormous value to subsequent artists and historians. They helped in incalculable ways to lift the spirits of a depressed nation and add to its culture. The WPA as a whole, like its arts projects, was certainly not without serious flaws, but the frequent complaint that it was nothing more than an attempt to provide 'bread and circuses' [distracting entertainment] is unjustified. The WPA proved, in fact, to be one of the leading examples of government recognition of the [democratic] values of Depression America."

the 1930s or inspired by New Deal policies provide low-cost loans to help individuals get started as home owners and small business proprietors. They shelter needy families in subsidized public housing at minimal cost. They protect and insure money deposited in banks. And agencies such as the National Endowment for the Arts (NEA) provide federal funding for the arts.

A second aspect of the New Deal's legacy can be seen in its lasting physical creations. The New Deal, in this regard, quite literally changed the American landscape.

These physical and tangible changes include the massive hydroelectric projects of Boulder, Bonneville, and Grand Coulee Dams. Other examples of major features are the hundred-mile-long causeway connecting Key West to the Florida mainland and the Triborough Bridge in New York City.

Millions of people today use parks, post offices, government buildings, airports, and other projects built by WPA labor. Lovers of wilderness enjoy vast tracts of national parks and forestland that were preserved by the CCC. The brilliant painting and writing created by the Federal One artists endure. The TVA and the Rural Electrification Administration, moreover, dramatically transformed America's farmland and changed the lives of millions.

A third aspect of the New Deal's legacy is less tangible—that is, it cannot be seen or touched, and it cannot always be observed in specific laws or agencies. This is the New Deal's outlook toward government in daily life, a philosophy that aimed at achieving humanitarian goals democratically.

Roosevelt passionately believed that every citizen is entitled to a decent standard of living; he also believed that government has a moral obligation to help those in need. In part through sheer strength of will, in part because of the desperate times, FDR was able to persuade a majority of the nation—and a majority of its legislators—to support his beliefs.

FDR's ideas were not new. In many ways, they reflected the progressive policies advocated earlier by Roosevelt's relative and mentor, Theodore Roosevelt. During the New Deal, these humanitarian ideals for the first time took on political shape and weight in the form of laws, agencies, and government policies. Using these new sets of rules, labor, minorities, and other groups were able to create a political coalition resulting in a Democratic Party that dominated national politics for most of the remaining century.

Furthermore, Roosevelt's liberal spirit has influenced several reform efforts in the years since the New Deal. The Great Society and the civil rights movement of the 1960s are two examples of agendas that reflected the ideals FDR summarized in his first inaugural address: "We aim at the assurance of a rounded, permanent national life."[100]

A Controversial Legacy

During its time, the New Deal never lacked critics on either end of the political spectrum. Today the programs and political atmosphere that the era created are still controversial.

Franklin and Eleanor Roosevelt greet well-wishers during a parade. Even today, FDR's presidency remains controversial: modern critics continue to debate the value of his New Deal programs.

Unfinished Work

In an essay in Franklin D. Roosevelt: His Life and Times, edited by Otis L. Graham Jr. and Meghan Robinson Wander, historian Graham reflects on FDR's belief that much of his reform work remained unfinished. (The Italian poet Dante was the author of The Inferno, *a classic allegory depicting the punishments in store for sinners of every description.)*

"In private, FDR mixed the satisfaction of achievement with disappointment that the New Deal system had not come closer to his intentions. But he often acknowledged its flaws as democracy's price. Obstacles could not be simply overpowered, as in closed societies; like the sailor he was, Roosevelt had been forced to tack toward harbor but had not yet made it by the time war intervened.

Historians refer to the developments of 1933–38 as 'the New Deal,' but Roosevelt in 1944 and 1945 was talking with friends about how much of the New Deal was yet undone. After the war, he said, there must be renewed efforts to achieve resource and public works planning, more river valley authorities, perhaps even a third, liberal party. In the meantime, shortcomings should be noted in the spirit of a remark he made in 1936, so often quoted:

The immortal Dante tells us that divine justice weighs the sins of the coldblooded and the sins of the warmhearted in different scales. Better the occasional faults of a government that lives in a spirit of charity than the constant omissions of a government frozen in the idea of its own indifference."

Conservatives in the 1930s claimed that government intervention crippled the economy and disrupted the freedoms of citizens. They argued that welfare and public works projects turned hardworking, self-reliant people into lazy idlers reliant on government handouts. They also objected to the concentration of power in the nation's capital and especially in the office of the president. They argued that FDR came dangerously close to creating a dictatorship, in which the government controlled virtually every aspect of life in a nation founded on the concept of individual freedom.

Some critics today fault FDR and the New Deal for what they see as hardened public perceptions of entitlement to welfare, Social Security, disability benefits, and so on. They also cite public acceptance of pervasive government regulation as a long-term legacy of FDR's decision, during World War II, to seek unprecedented powers for himself and for federal agencies.

Many people, including some admirers of FDR, agree that government intervention in everyday life has grown by leaps and bounds in the decades since the end of the depression. These people come from all across the political spectrum: Democrats and Republicans who work for change from within the system, libertarians who advocate deregulation in almost every aspect of life, and extremists in private militias who reject the authority of the federal government to tax them or otherwise regulate their lives. Thoughtful people from all these camps worry about what one conservative commentator, John Willson, calls "an expansion of the national state so vast as to be virtually irreversible."[101]

On Balance

Some liberals, although generally in sympathy with New Deal ideas, have also criticized Roosevelt. They complain that FDR did not reform government enough. They say he was content to enact small reforms, instead of promoting sweeping changes that would have lessened the gaps in opportunity and standards of living between rich and poor.

They also charge that his administration did not seriously confront problems of racial and sexual inequality. Although New Dealers appointed more blacks and women to important government posts than minority groups and women had ever held before, liberal critics contend that the New Deal did not ensure equal opportunity for all.

For better or worse, many aspects of the New Deal have become an apparently permanent part of the national fabric. Roosevelt may have fallen short of his complete set of goals for the New Deal. He did much, however, to change a depressed nation's mood from gloom to hope, he continued to maintain that optimism during times of global crisis, and he instituted many important changes in America's social structure. In so doing, FDR set the standard for future activists and lawmakers who admire the New Deal and who emulate Roosevelt's combination of robust energy, astute political sense, and tireless social conscience.

Appendix

Major New Deal Agencies and Legislation

AAA: Agricultural Adjustment Administration, 1933. Administered many farm and agricultural programs, including the controversial crop subsidy program.

CCC: Civilian Conservation Corps, 1933. Provided work for young men in national parks and the wilderness.

CWA: Civil Works Administration, 1933. A forerunner of more extensive works projects agencies such as the **PWA** and **WPA.**

FDIC: Federal Deposit Insurance Corporation, 1933. Insured individual bank deposits to prevent runs on banks by investors.

FERA: Federal Emergency Relief Administration, 1933. One of the first relief agencies of the New Deal, designed to provide emergency money to needy families.

FHA: Federal Housing Administration, 1934. Established low-interest loans for first-time home buyers.

NLRB: National Labor Relations Board, 1934–35. Created to mediate disputes peacefully between representatives of labor and industry.

NRA: National Recovery Administration, 1933. Attempted to establish standards and codes for business and industry. Only partly successful, dissolved in 1935.

NYA: National Youth Administration, 1935. Employed young men and women in work-study jobs to aid in their further education.

PWA: Public Works Administration, 1933. Large-scale works projects agency, responsible for many major projects such as highways and dams.

REA: Rural Electrification Administration, 1935. An extension of the TVA's program to bring electricity in cheap, readily available quantities to rural America.

SEC: Securities and Exchange Commission, 1934. Created to oversee and regulate the buying and selling of stocks and bonds, curbing the reckless and unethical practices that had caused the Crash of 1929.

SSA: Social Security Act, 1935. Established the Social Security Administration, the first national unemployment and retirement insurance program.

TVA: Tennessee Valley Authority, 1933. The first and largest rural electrification program, creating hydroelectric power in seven states along the Tennessee River.

WPA: Works Progress Administration, 1935. The largest of the federal works projects programs, responsible for a wide variety of activities ranging from the construction of public office buildings to federally funded arts programs. Name changed in 1939 to Work Projects Administration.

Notes

Introduction: A New Deal for America

1. Quoted in Studs Terkel, *Hard Times*. New York: Pantheon Books, 1970, p. 39.
2. Quoted in William E. Leuchtenberg, *Franklin D. Roosevelt and the New Deal*. New York: Harper and Row, 1963, p. 330.
3. Quoted in Leuchtenberg, *Franklin D. Roosevelt and the New Deal*, p. 326.

Chapter 1: Before the New Deal: The Great Depression

4. Quoted in Anthony J. Badger, *The New Deal*. New York: Noonday Press/Farrar, Straus, and Giroux, 1989, p. 29.
5. Leuchtenberg, *Franklin D. Roosevelt and the New Deal*, p. 26.
6. Quoted in Leuchtenberg, *Franklin D. Roosevelt and the New Deal*, p. 13.
7. Words and music by E. Harburg and J. Gorney, copyright 1932, Harms, Inc.
8. Quoted in Ted Morgan, *FDR: A Biography*. New York: Simon and Schuster, 1985, p. 319.
9. Quoted in Badger, *The New Deal*, p. 36.
10. Quoted in Leuchtenberg, *Franklin D. Roosevelt and the New Deal*, p. 13.
11. Badger, *The New Deal*, p. 53.
12. Page Smith, *Redeeming the Time: A People's History of the 1920s and the New Deal*. New York: McGraw-Hill, 1987, p. 456.
13. Frank Freidel, *Franklin D. Roosevelt: A Rendezvous with Destiny*. Boston: Little, Brown, 1990, p. 60.
14. Quoted in Freidel, *Franklin D. Roosevelt: A Rendezvous with Destiny*, p. 61.
15. Quoted in Smith, *Redeeming the Time*, pp. 326–27.
16. Quoted in Smith, *Redeeming the Time*, p. 334.
17. Quoted in Freidel, *Franklin D. Roosevelt: A Rendezvous with Destiny*, p. 47.
18. Shelley Bookspan, "Interregnum," in Otis L. Graham Jr. and Meghan Robinson Wander, eds., *Franklin D. Roosevelt: His Life and Times: An Encyclopedic View*. New York: Da Capo Press, 1985, p. 210.

Chapter 2: "The Only Thing We Have to Fear Is Fear Itself": The New Deal Is Born

19. Robert S. McElvaine, *The Great Depression*. New York: Times Books, 1984, p. 123.
20. Quoted in *Time*, Oct. 5, 1983, p. 101.
21. Badger, *The New Deal*, p. 67.
22. Quoted in Badger, *The New Deal*, p. 71.
23. Quoted in Smith, *Redeeming the Time*, p. 438.
24. Quoted in Katie Loucheim, ed., *The Making of the New Deal*. Cambridge, MA: Harvard University Press, 1983, p. 225.
25. Quoted in Leuchtenberg, *Franklin D. Roosevelt and the New Deal*, p. 192.
26. Freidel, *Franklin D. Roosevelt: A Rendezvous with Destiny*, p. 92.
27. Quoted in Morgan, *FDR: A Biography*, p. 375.
28. Freidel, *Franklin D. Roosevelt: A Rendezvous with Destiny*, p. 99.
29. Quoted in Morgan, *FDR: A Biography*, p. 377.
30. William E. Leuchtenberg, *The FDR Years: On Roosevelt and His Legacy*. New York: Columbia University Press, 1995, p. 49.
31. Quoted in Loucheim, ed., *The Making of the New Deal*, p. 300.
32. Quoted in McElvaine, *The Great Depression*, p. 138.
33. Quoted in Robert Bendiner, *Just Around the Corner*. New York: Harper and Row, 1967, p. 35.

Chapter 3: Programs for Farming and Industry

34. Quoted in Freidel, *Franklin D. Roosevelt: A Rendezvous with Destiny,* p. 126.

35. Quoted in Terkel, *Hard Times,* p. 218.

36. McElvaine, *The Great Depression,* p. 149.

37. Quoted in Terkel, *Hard Times,* p. 219.

38. McElvaine, *The Great Depression,* p. 158.

39. Quoted in Morgan, *FDR: A Biography,* p. 388.

40. Quoted in Leuchtenberg, *Franklin D. Roosevelt and the New Deal,* p. 66.

41. Quoted in Morgan, *FDR: A Biography,* p. 401.

42. Ellis W. Hawley, "National Recovery Administration," in Graham and Wander, eds., *Franklin D. Roosevelt: His Life and Times: An Encyclopedic View,* p. 274.

43. Hawley, "National Recovery Administration," in Graham and Wander, eds., *Franklin D. Roosevelt: His Life and Times: An Encyclopedic View,* p. 275.

Chapter 4: Programs for Relief, Works Projects, and More

44. Quoted in Badger, *The New Deal,* p. 33.

45. Quoted in Morgan, *FDR: A Biography,* p. 321.

46. Quoted in McElvaine, *The Great Depression,* p. 152.

47. Quoted in Freidel, *Franklin D. Roosevelt: A Rendezvous with Destiny,* p. 135.

48. Quoted in McElvaine, *The Great Depression,* p. 153.

49. Quoted in Morgan, *FDR: A Biography,* p. 389.

50. Quoted in John Salmond, "National Youth Administration," in Graham and Wander, eds., *Franklin D. Roosevelt: His Life and Times: An Encyclopedic View,* pp. 278–79.

51. Smith, *Redeeming the Time,* p. 440.

52. Freidel, *Franklin D. Roosevelt: A Rendezvous with Destiny,* p. 157.

53. Leuchtenberg, *Franklin D. Roosevelt and the New Deal,* p. 54.

54. Quoted in McElvaine, *The Great Depression,* pp. 157–58.

55. John Muldowny, "Rural Electrification Administration," in Graham and Wander, eds., *Franklin D. Roosevelt: His Life and Times: An Encyclopedic View,* p. 379.

56. Badger, *The New Deal,* p. 71.

Chapter 5: A Second New Deal

57. Quoted in McElvaine, *The Great Depression,* p. 253.

58. Quoted in Leuchtenberg, *Franklin D. Roosevelt and the New Deal,* p. 117.

59. Otis L Graham, "New Deal," in Graham and Wander, eds., *Franklin D. Roosevelt: His Life and Times: An Encyclopedic View,* p. 290.

60. Quoted in Smith, *Redeeming the Time,* p. 612.

61. Quoted in Richard D. McKinzie, "Federal Art Project," in Graham and Wander, eds., *Franklin D. Roosevelt: His Life and Times: An Encyclopedic View,* p. 128.

62. Freidel, *Franklin D. Roosevelt: A Rendezvous with Destiny,* p. 188.

63. Bendiner, *Just Around the Corner,* pp. 194–95.

64. Quoted in McElvaine, *The Great Depression,* p. 272.

65. Smith, *Redeeming the Time,* p. 798.

66. McElvaine, *The Great Depression,* p. 271.

67. Searle F. Charles, "Relief," in Graham and Wander, eds., *Franklin D. Roosevelt: His Life and Times: An Encyclopedic View,* p. 353.

Chapter 6: Social Security, Sick Chickens, and a Second Term of Office

68. Quoted in W. Andrew Achenbaum, "Social Security," in Graham and Wander, eds., *Franklin D. Roosevelt: His Life and Times: An Encyclopedic View,* p. 391.

69. Quoted in Morgan, *FDR: A Biography*, p. 424.

70. McElvaine, *The Great Depression*, p. 257.

71. Quoted in Leuchtenberg, *Franklin D. Roosevelt and the New Deal*, p. 145.

72. Quoted in Freidel, *Franklin D. Roosevelt: A Rendezvous with Destiny*, p. 161.

73. Quoted in McElvaine, *The Great Depression*, p. 162.

74. Quoted in Morgan, *FDR: A Biography*, p. 428.

75. Quoted in Leuchtenberg, *The FDR Years: On Roosevelt and His Legacy*, p. 92.

76. Quoted in Smith, *Redeeming the Time*, pp. 674–75.

Chapter 7: The War Arrives, the New Deal Ends

77. Quoted in Kenneth S. Davis, *FDR: Into the Storm, 1937–1940*. New York: Random House, 1986, p. 42.

78. McElvaine, *The Great Depression*, p. 284.

79. Freidel, *Franklin D. Roosevelt: A Rendezvous with Destiny*, p. 222.

80. Quoted in Davis, *FDR: Into the Storm, 1937–1940*, p. 44.

81. Quoted in Smith, *Redeeming the Time*, p. 685.

82. Quoted in Davis, *FDR: Into the Storm, 1937–1940*, pp. 65–66.

83. McElvaine, *The Great Depression*, p. 286.

84. Freidel, *Franklin D. Roosevelt: A Rendezvous with Destiny*, p. 275.

85. Quoted in Morgan, *FDR: A Biography*, p. 493.

86. Quoted in Freidel, *Franklin D. Roosevelt: A Rendezvous with Destiny*, p. 280.

87. Nelson Lichtenstein, "Labor," quoted in Graham and Wander, eds., *Franklin D. Roosevelt: His Life and Times: An Encyclopedic View*, p. 227.

88. Quoted in Leuchtenberg, *Franklin D. Roosevelt and the New Deal*, p. 112.

89. Quoted in Smith, *Redeeming the Time*, p. 754.

90. Quoted in Leuchtenberg, *Franklin D. Roosevelt and the New Deal*, p. 263.

91. Quoted in Morgan, *FDR: A Biography*, p. 493.

92. Smith, *Redeeming the Time*, p. 803.

93. Quoted in Morgan, *FDR: A Biography*, p. 664.

94. W. Elliot Brownlee, "Recession of 1937–38," in Graham and Wander, eds., *Franklin D. Roosevelt: His Life and Times: An Encyclopedic View*, p. 347.

95. Leuchtenberg, *The FDR Years: On Roosevelt and His Legacy*, p. 224.

96. Quoted in Freidel, *Franklin D. Roosevelt: A Rendezvous with Destiny*, p. 249.

97. Quoted in John Willson, "How World War II Saved the New Deal," *USA Today* (magazine), July 1993.

98. Quoted in Freidel, *Franklin D. Roosevelt: A Rendezvous with Destiny*, p. 500.

Epilogue: Assessing the New Deal

99. Alan Brinkley, "The New Deal," in Eric Foner and John A. Garraty, eds., *The Reader's Companion to American History*. Boston: Houghton Mifflin, 1991, p. 783.

100. Franklin D. Roosevelt, *Looking Forward*. New York: John Day, 1933, p. 269.

101. John Willson, "How World War II Saved the New Deal," July 1993.

For Further Reading

William Dudley, ed., *The Great Depression*. San Diego: Greenhaven Press, 1994. This title in the Opposing Viewpoints series presents carefully chosen excerpts from writings, including first-hand accounts, about the event that helped bring the New Deal into being.

Russell Freedman, *Franklin Delano Roosevelt*. New York: Clarion Books, 1990. A well-written biography that clearly traces FDR's rise to prominence, with excellent photographic illustrations.

Edmund Lindop, *The Turbulent Thirties*. New York: Franklin Watts, 1970. A good introduction to the thirties in America, including sections on the movies, music, and sports as well as on the political and social events of the period.

Anne E. Schraff, *The Great Depression and the New Deal*. New York: Franklin Watts, 1990. A good introduction, written for high school students, to the depression and New Deal policies.

Gail B. Stewart, *The New Deal*. New York: New Discovery/Macmillan, 1993. A simply written, basic introduction to New Deal programs, with some good photo illustrations.

Works Consulted

Joseph Alsop, *FDR: A Centenary Remembrance.* New York: Viking Press, 1982. Not a full biography, but a book-length essay by a veteran political columnist. A large-format book with excellent photos.

Anthony J. Badger, *The New Deal.* New York: Noonday Press/Farrar, Straus, and Giroux, 1989. A densely written work that focuses on the policies, not the personality, of FDR, by a British professor of American history.

Robert Bendiner, *Just Around the Corner.* New York: Harper and Row, 1967. A lively, anecdotal history of the thirties.

John Braeman, Robert H. Bremner, and David Brody, eds., *The New Deal.* Columbus: Ohio State University Press, 1975. A collection of scholarly articles by university professors on various aspects of the New Deal.

George J. Church, "The Wealth of Nations," *Time,* October 5, 1983. A magazine piece commemorating the fiftieth anniversary of *Time.*

Pete Daniel, Merry A. Foresta, Maren Strange, and Sally Stein, *Official Images: New Deal Photography.* Washington, DC: Smithsonian Institution Press, 1987. A fascinating collection of photos from the WPA, NYA, CCC, and other New Deal–era agencies. Includes many images by such famous photographers as Walker Evans, Dorothea Lange, and Edward Weston.

Kenneth S. Davis, *FDR: Into the Storm, 1937–1940.* New York: Random House, 1986. One volume of a multivolume work by a distinguished biographer. Written in a heavy, florid style, it is difficult to read smoothly but well researched and full of factual information.

Eric Foner and John A. Garraty, eds., *The Reader's Companion to American History.* Boston: Houghton Mifflin, 1991. A valuable collection of brief articles written by a number of prominent historians.

Frank Freidel, *Franklin D. Roosevelt: A Rendezvous with Destiny.* Boston: Little, Brown, 1990. An excellent one-volume version of the author's definitive multivolume biography of FDR. Perhaps the best single book on the subject, written by a distinguished Harvard professor of history.

Doris Kearns Goodwin, *No Ordinary Time.* New York: Simon and Schuster, 1994. An excellent book by one of the finest popular American historians. Though it concentrates on the Roosevelt family during the Second World War, it has small sections on the New Deal.

Otis L. Graham Jr. and Meghan Robinson Wander, eds., *Franklin D. Roosevelt: His Life and Times: An Encyclopedic View.*

New York: Da Capo Press, 1985. An extremely useful and thorough book, with clear and concise articles, by a variety of scholars and historians, on many aspects of FDR and the New Deal. An excellent resource.

William E. Leuchtenberg, *The FDR Years: On Roosevelt and His Legacy.* New York: Columbia University Press, 1995. A collection of essays that distills and amplifies the points made in the author's many works on Roosevelt and the New Deal.

———, *Franklin D. Roosevelt and the New Deal.* New York: Harper and Row, 1963. A classic work by a leading expert on New Deal history. This volume, part of the New American Nation series, is informative, clearly written, and enlivened with many quotations.

———, ed., *The New Deal: A Documentary History.* New York: Harper and Row, 1968. A thoughtful collection of writings from the New Deal era by a variety of journalists, poets, novelists, playwrights, and essayists, including many who were part of FDR's inner circle.

Katie Loucheim, ed., *The Making of the New Deal.* Cambridge, MA: Harvard University Press, 1983. An anthology of lively, anecdotal reminiscences by a variety of individuals who took part in the shaping of Roosevelt's various New Deal programs.

Robert S. McElvaine, *The Great Depression.* New York: Times Books, 1984. A lively survey of America during 1929–1941, by a history professor who places an emphasis on the depression's effect on ordinary, working-class citizens.

Ted Morgan, *FDR: A Biography.* New York: Simon and Schuster, 1985. A thorough and well-written account by a well-known biographer.

Franklin D. Roosevelt, *Looking Forward.* New York: John Day, 1933. A collection of essays, articles, and speeches by FDR on a number of topics related to the New Deal.

Arthur M. Schlesinger Jr., *The Coming of the New Deal.* Boston: Houghton Mifflin, 1958. Part of the trilogy of books The Age of Roosevelt. Densely written and difficult to follow, but nonetheless considered one of the classic texts on Roosevelt and the New Deal.

———, *The Politics of Upheaval.* Boston: Houghton Mifflin, 1958. The third volume of The Age of Roosevelt. Schlesinger, an eminent historian, is considered by some observers to be biased too far in favor of FDR's policies, but this is an essential work nonetheless.

Page Smith, *Redeeming the Time: A People's History of the 1920s and the New Deal.* New York: McGraw-Hill, 1987. An extremely thorough book by a prominent historian, with an emphasis on the lives of ordinary people as well as the events that affected them.

Studs Terkel, *Hard Times.* New York: Pantheon Books, 1970. A wonderful book of oral history about the depression by ordinary people who lived through it, by a distinguished radio interviewer and writer.

Rexford G. Tugwell, *FDR: Architect of an Era.* New York: Macmillan, 1967. A biography by one of the key members of the Brain Trust. Biased toward the positive—Tugwell was a close friend as well as an adviser of FDR's—but clearly written and well illustrated with photos.

United States Supreme Court, *U.S. Reports,* vol. 295. Washington, DC: Government Printing Office, 1935. This is the volume of official Supreme Court rulings that contains the "sick chicken" ruling declaring the NIRA unconstitutional.

John Willson, "How World War II Saved the New Deal," *USA Today* (magazine), July 1993. A brief article by a contemporary conservative commentator.

Index

Picture Credits

Cover photo: Corbis-Bettmann

Archive Photos, 13 (bottom), 81, 85, 90, 95

Corbis-Bettmann, 19 (right), 64

FDR Library, 72

Library of Congress, 10, 13 (top), 15, 16, 18, 19 (left), 21 (both), 22, 24, 26, 28, 30, 36, 42, 45, 46, 50, 53, 54, 55, 56, 62, 66, 68, 71, 74, 76, 82, 84, 88

National Archives, 31, 34, 51, 65, 92, 97

Stock Montage, Inc., 44

UPI/Corbis-Bettmann, 32, 48, 77, 80, 86

About the Author

Adam Woog has written many books for children, young adults, and adults, including over a dozen titles for Lucent Books. He lives with his wife and young daughter in Seattle, Washington.